# THE COUNTRYSIDE QUIZ

All sorts of wonderful and exciting things happen in the countryside as the seasons pass by. This Quiz has been written to help you to enjoy and understand how the countryside and its inhabitants change throughout the year.

For instance, do you know what wild flowers you would be likely to see in the Summer, or which animals hibernate during the Winter months? Can you recognise the birds who arrive with the Spring or tell the difference between a Frog and a Toad? These are just a few of the questions asked by the Countryside Quiz—the answers are fascinating.

Explore Britain's lovely countryside as soon as possible, and take this book with you— it will open up a thrilling and beautiful world to you.

3 cde

Other CAROUSEL books by MALCOLM SAVILLE

EAT WHAT YOU GROW
JANE'S COUNTRY YEAR
MALCOLM SAVILLE'S COUNTRY BOOK
MALCOLM SAVILLE'S SEASIDE BOOK

Also by MALCOLM SAVILLE

THE WONDER WHY BOOK OF
EXPLORING A WOOD

# The Countryside Quiz

by

## Malcolm Saville

Illustrated by Robert Micklewright

**CAROUSEL BOOKS**
A DIVISION OF TRANSWORLD PUBLISHERS LTD

THE COUNTRYSIDE QUIZ
A CORGI CAROUSEL BOOK 0 552 54133 8

First publication in Great Britain

PRINTING HISTORY

Corgi Carousel edition published 1978

Text copyright © Malcolm Saville 1978
Illustrations copyright © Transworld Publishers 1978



This book is set in Monotype Baskerville 12/13 pt.

Carousel Books are published by Transworld Publishers Ltd.,
Century House, 61–63 Uxbridge Road, Ealing,
London, W5 5SA.

Made and Printed in Great Britain by
Richard Clay (The Chaucer Press), Ltd., Bungay, Suffolk

# CONTENTS

# Introduction

This book is to help you to enjoy all the wonderful and exciting experiences which our countryside has to offer. You may think that the country is quiet. So it is, compared with our towns and cities, but if you keep your eyes and ears open it is a great deal more exciting. I wonder if you realise that people from all parts of the world come to Britain to explore our lovely land? They come to see our woods and forests, our rivers and lakes, our mountains and gentle hills. I live near the sea in the glorious county of Sussex, so we are among the first to see the birds who come back to Britain each Spring. Do **you** know which birds fly thousands of kilometres to come to us? Turn to page 13 and see if you can answer the quiz about what we call 'migrant birds'. Or better still go into the country in the Spring and see how many birds you can recognise. Do you know what wild flowers you would be likely to see in a wood in Summer? Turn to page 44 and use your wits before you look up the answers. It is better to see, to learn and remember, than it is to guess. And how many wild animals have you actually **seen** in the country? Would you know a **Dormouse** if you saw one? What is the difference between a **Frog** and a **Toad**? What tree is called **The Queen of the Forest** and what birds would you be likely to see on the farmer's fields when he is ploughing?

These are the sort of questions this book will answer for you. I have tried to make it fun to read and the artist has drawn many superb pictures, which will help you to remember what you saw.

I hope you will also like to read a few verses written by famous poets who loved the country. So do I, and have written two books (both in paperback) which will tell you more than I have had room to do here. If you would like to know more about them write to me at this address: Malcolm Saville, Chelsea Cottage, Winchelsea, East Sussex TN36 4HU.

# SPRING

Have you ever thought how wonderful are the four seasons of the year? Have you wondered how, and even why, they happen? Nobody can begin to imagine what our lives would be without Spring, Summer, Autumn and Winter. Understanding and watching how the seasons pass is easier in the country-side because you can see it happening, and so I have planned this Quiz in four sections so that you can follow them through the year.

Spring often comes with, what a poet described so beautifully as 'hurrying feet'. Suddenly, there comes a day, usually in March, when a gentle west wind clears the skies and the sun warms the new-born lambs, and we can hear the birds singing again as they busy themselves in trees and hedgerows and gardens with their home-making. Then we can say that winter is behind us, and I hope that you, now reading these words, and some of the poems on the following pages which I have found for you, will realise that the coming of Spring is the greatest miracle of all. Get out into the country as soon as you can and take this book with you and watch the world being born again.

See the farmer's fields. He will have ploughed many of these in Autumn, and now they will be tinged with green. Watch the rooks squabbling and cawing about their untidy nests in the tree-tops. Look for violets and primroses in hedgerows and if you can find a stream or a pond and watch carefully, you will see new life there.

Be happy in Spring.

# Winter and Spring

*But a little while ago*
*All the ground was white with snow;*
*Trees and shrubs were dry and bare,*
*Not a sign of life was there;*
*Now the buds and leaves are seen,*
*Now the fields are fresh and green,*
*Pretty birds are on the wing,*
*With a merry song they sing!*
*There's new life in everything!*
*How I love the pleasant spring!*

**William Wordsworth**

# SPRING QUIZ

# Spring Song

*Up, up, let us greet*
*The season so sweet,*
*For winter is gone,*
*And the flowers are springing*
*And little birds singing,*
*Their soft notes ringing,*
*And bright is the sun!*
*Where all was dressed*
*In a snowy vest,*
*There grass is growing*
*With dew-drops glowing,*
*And flowers are seen*
*On beds of green.*

**Q.** Godfrey of Nifen, who wrote that poem, lived in the thirteenth century. When did the thirteenth century begin and when did it end?

**1.** There are thirteen birds in this list:

> **Swallow**
> **Swift**
> **Eagle**
> **Cuckoo**
> **House Martin**
> **Nightingale**
> **Parrot**
> **Yellow Wagtail**
> **Lesser Whitethroat**
> **Robin**
> **Willow Warbler**
> **Turtle Dove**
> **Canary**

Of the thirteen, nine are birds that each year fly thousands of kilometres from other countries to nest somewhere in the British Isles. Can you spot the nine?

If you are stuck you can get some help by turning the page. There you will find an illustration of each of the nine birds. See how many of them you recognise.

14

**2.** This is a bird that lays its eggs in other birds' nests:

What is it called?

**3.** This is a brightly-coloured bird that makes its nests in the holes in the trunks of trees:

What is it called?

**4.** In the early Spring this bird returns to the nest it built last year:

What is the bird called?

**5.** One of these names is the name for a rook's nest:

**A Rockery**
**A Rooknest**
**A Rookcot**
**A Nestie**
**A Nookery**
**A Rookery**
**An Eerie**
**A Dovecote**
**A Rook's Den**
**A Rookout**

Which one?

**6.** Here are six groups of birds:

a. **Pigeons**
   **Pheasants**
   **Partridges**

b. **Ducks**
   **Geese**
   **Turkeys**

c. **Gulls**
   **Lapwings***
   **Rooks**

d. **Starlings**
   **Robins**
   **Chaffinches**

e. **Wrens**
   **Tits**
   **Jackdaws**

f. **Swallows**
   **Larks**
   **Cuckoos**

* The **Lapwing** is also known as **Peewit** and **Green Plover**

Of the six groups of birds, which one would you expect to see most often on a newly-ploughed field in the Spring?

**7.** There are thirteen trees named in this list:

Alder
Poplar
Sweet Chestnut
Birch
Oak
Larch
Holly
Linden
Pine
Horse-Chestnut
Ash
Cherry
Laburnum

Of the thirteen, five are trees that bear **catkins.**
Can you spot the five trees in the list that have
catkins?

The five trees are illustrated on the next page.
Can you name each one of them?

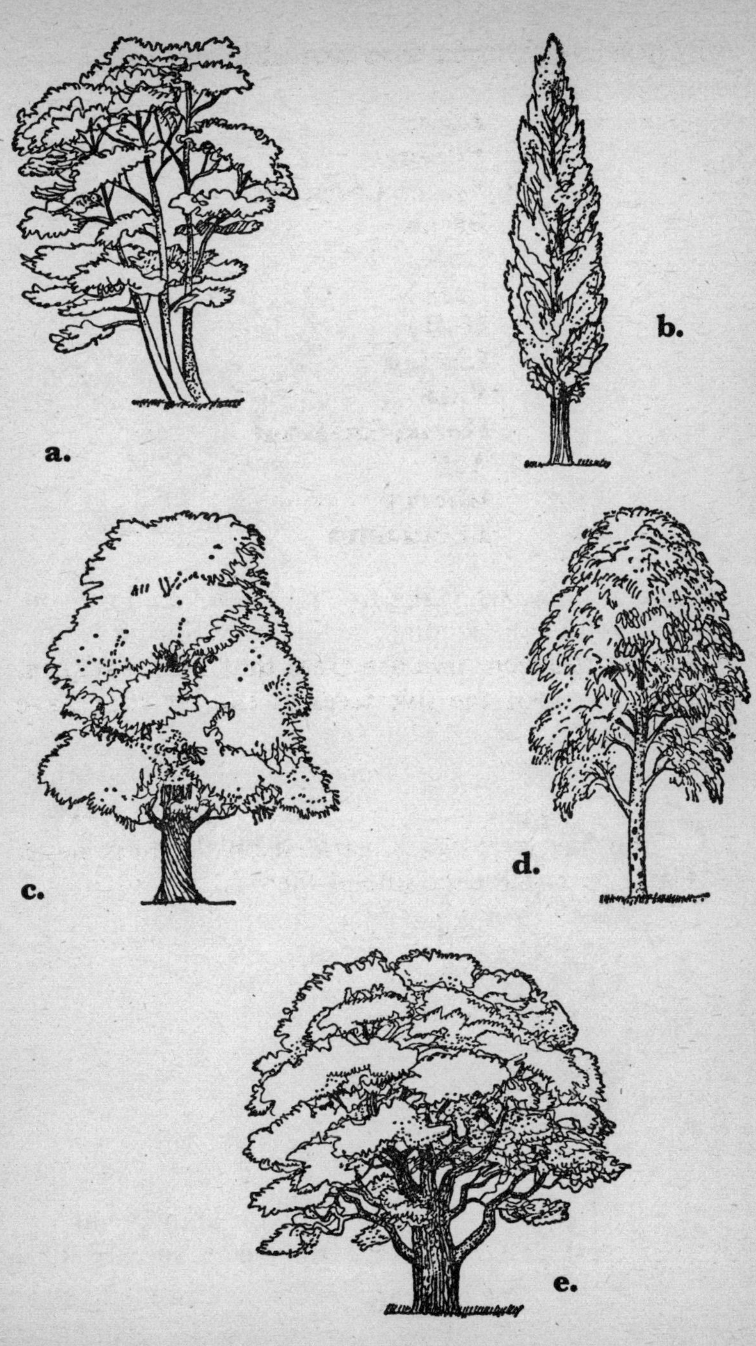

a.
b.
c.
d.
e.

**8.** In the early Spring this
tree looks pink:

Do you know what the tree is called? And do you
know why it looks pink in the early Spring?

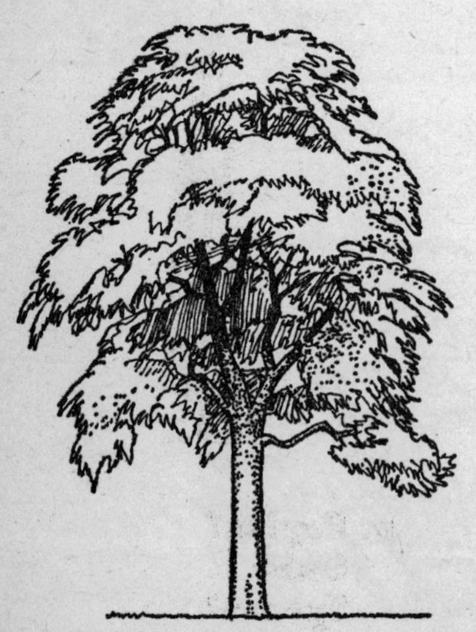

**9.** This tree is one of the
last to open its leaves
in Spring:

Do you know what
the tree is called?

**10.** This is a well-known Christmas decoration:

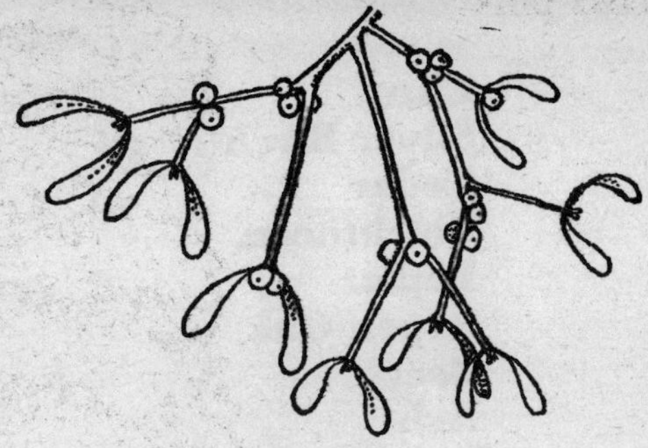

**Is it Holly?**
**Is it Ivy?**
**Is it Mistletoe?**

Whichever it is, you will find that it flowers in March and grows on another tree. Here are two of the trees on which it can usually be found in the Spring. What are they?

**a. Apple?**
**Cherry?**
**Pear?**

**b. Poplar?**
**Oak?**
**Spruce?**

**11.** Here are the names of fifteen famous shrubs and trees:

> **Elm**
> **Silver Birch**
> **Cedar**
> **Blackthorn**
> **Poplar**
> **Aspen Oak**
> **Beech**
> **Ash**
> **Fir**
> **Willow**
> **Larch**
> **Wild Cherry**
> **Horse-Chestnut**
> **Hawthorn**
> **Walnut**

Of the fifteen, only twelve blossom in the Spring.

Can you spot the twelve?

**12.** Here are pictures of three famous trees:

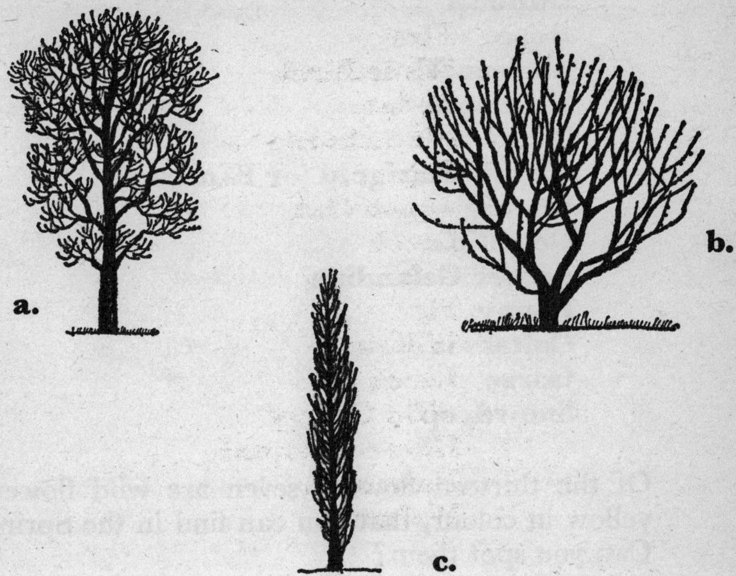

Do you know what the three trees are called?

And do you know what the three trees have in common?

> **a. Are they all trees that have flowers before leaves?**
>
> **b. Are they all trees that flourish in the tropics?**
>
> **c. Are they all trees that have been hit by Dutch Elm disease?**
>
> **d. Are they all conifers?**

**13.** Here are the names of thirteen flowers:

**Daffodil**
**Rose**
**African Violet**
**Primrose**
**Tulip**
**Marsh Marigold (or Kingcup)**
**Orchid**
**Cowslip**
**Lesser Celandine**
**Poppy**
**Coltsfoot**
**Gorse**
**Snowdrop**

Of the thirteen flowers, seven are wild flowers, yellow in colour, that you can find in the Spring. Can you spot them?

To help you, you will find all seven flowers illustrated below and on the next page. Can you put a name to each one of them?

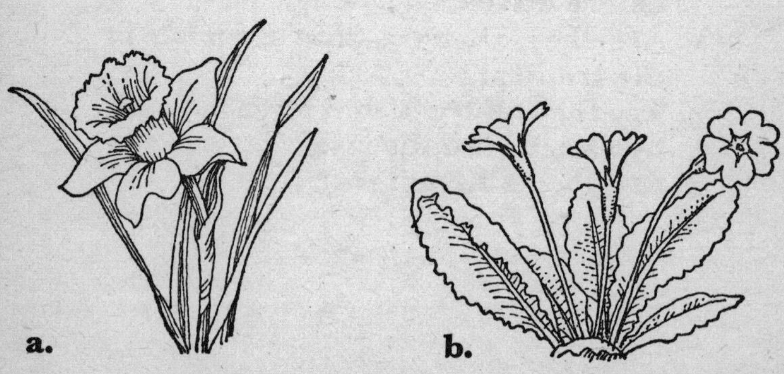

a.         b.

c.

d.

e.

f.

g.

**14.** This is a picture of one of the very first flowers of the year:
What is it called?

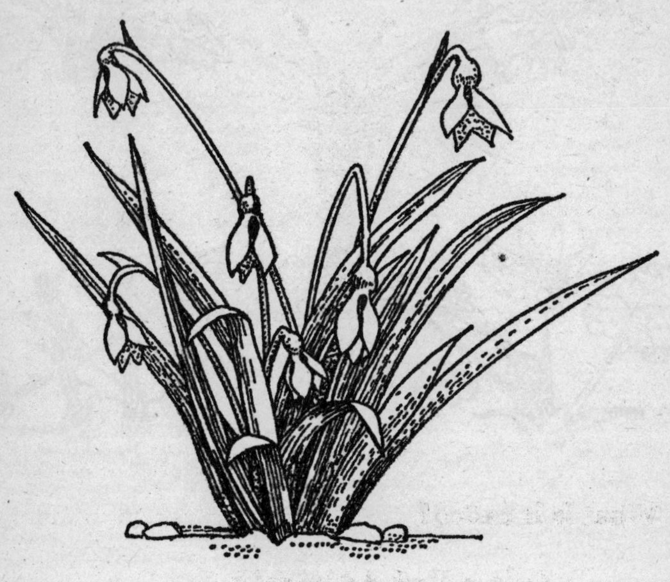

And do you know why it hangs its head?

    **a. Is it because it is weather-beaten?**
    **b. Is it because it is sad?**
    **c. Is it to protect its pollen from the rain and snow?**
    **d. Is it because it is about to flower?**

**15.** This is one of the first butterflies you will see in
the Spring:

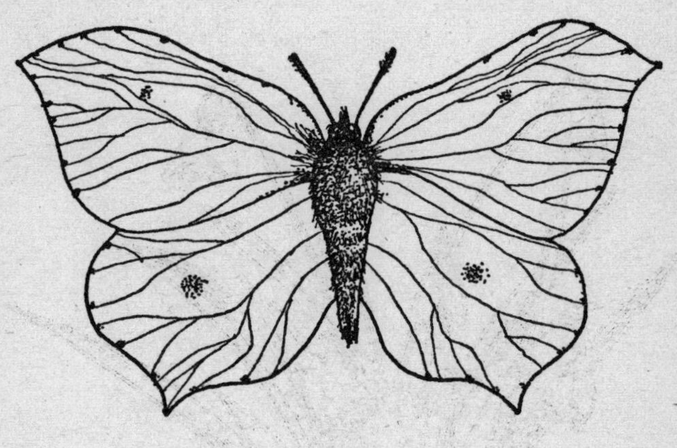

What is it called?

**Is it a Red Admiral?**
**Is it a Small Tortoiseshell?**
**Is it a Brimstone?**
**Is it a Peacock?**
**Is it an Orange Tip?**
**Is it a Large Copper?**
**Is it a Swallowtail?**

**16.** One of these creatures is a rabbit and one is a hare.

a.

b.

But which is which?

28

**17.** What is the correct name for a female fox?

Is it a foxette?
Is it a wolf?
Is it a vixen?
Is it a vole?
Is it a foxglove?
Is it a fefox?
Is it a foxtrot?

**18.** What is the correct name for a female rabbit?

Is it a dear rabbit?
Is it a bunny rabbit?
Is it a doe rabbit?
Is it a hare rabbit?
Is it a she rabbit?

**19.** What is the correct name for a male rabbit?

Is it a Welsh rabbit?
Is it a bull rabbit?
Is it a buck rabbit?
Is it a male rabbit?
Is it a stag rabbit?

**20.** Here is a list of eight animals and a list of the
names given to the young of those eight animals.
At the moment, the lists don't match. Can you sort
out the two lists and match the parents with their
young?

| The Parent | The Young |
| --- | --- |
| Fox | Lamb |
| Hare | Fawn |
| Sheep | Kid |
| Cow | Cub |
| Horse | Leveret |
| Goat | Calf |
| Deer | Foal |

**21.** These are the correct names for the homes of four
famous animals:

Burrow
Set
Earth
Drey

And these are the names of the four animals:

Fox
Rabbit
Squirrel
Badger

Which home belongs to which animal?

**22.** One of these animals is a **Stoat** and one is a
**Weasel**:

a.

b.

But which is which?

**23.** This little fish is known as a fierce and fearless fighter:

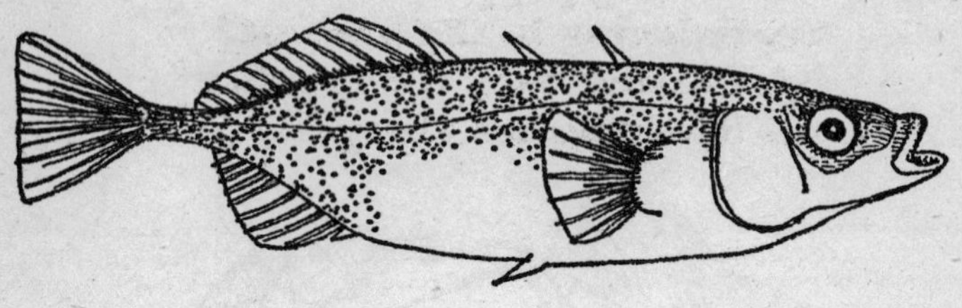

What is its name?

**24.** What are you likely to find in a pond in the Spring?

**Would you find seaweed?**
**Would you find goldfish eggs?**
**Would you find spring greens?**
**Would you find frogspawn?**
**Would you find jellyfish?**

**25.** Which of these jobs could you expect to see a farmer doing in February and March:

a. Sowing barley and oats?
b. Sowing poppies?
c. Bringing in the harvest?
d. Cutting back the bracken?
e. Shearing the sheep?

And which of these jobs would you expect to see a farmer doing in April:

f. Sowing potatoes and sugar beet?
g. Harvesting turnips and swedes?
h. Cutting back yellow toad-flax?
i. Building haystacks?

# Home Thoughts From Abroad

O, to be in England
    Now that April's there,
And whoever wakes in England
Sees, some morning, unaware,
That the lowest boughs and the brushwood sheaf
Round the elm-tree bole are in tiny leaf,
While the chaffinch sings on the orchard bough
In England—now!

And after April, when May follows,
And the whitethroat builds, and all the swallows!
Hark, where my blossom'd pear-tree in the hedge
Leans to the field and scatters on the clover
Blossoms and dewdrops—at the bent spray's edge—
That's the wise thrush; he sings each song twice over,
Lest you should think he never could recapture
The first fine careless rapture!
And though the fields look rough with hoary dew,
All will be agy when the noontide wakes anew
The buttercups, the little children's dower
—Far brighter than this gaudy melon-flower!

Robert Browning

# Answers to the Spring Quiz

1. a. Swallow        b. Swift
   c. Cuckoo        d. House Martin
   e. Nightingale     f. Yellow Wagtail
   g. Lesser Whitethroat   h. Willow Warbler
   i. Turtle Dove
2. A Cuckoo
3. A Woodpecker
4. The Rook
5. A Rookery
6. c. Gulls
      Lapwings
      Rooks
7. a. Alder            b. Poplar
   c. Sweet Chestnut   d. Birch
   e. Oak
8. The **Elm** and it looks pink in the early Spring because its flowers come out before its leaves.
9. The Ash
10. Mistletoe
      a. Apple
      b. Poplar
11. Elm           Ash
    Silver Birch   Willow
    Blackthorn    Larch
    Poplar        Wild Cherry
    Aspen Oak    Horse-Chestnut
    Beech         Hawthorn
12. a. Elm
    b. Sallow or Pussy Willow
    c. Poplar
    They are all trees that have flowers before they have leaves.

13. a. **Daffodil**               b. **Primrose**
    c. **Marsh Marigold**        d. **Cowslip**
       **or Kingcup**
    e. **Lesser Celandine**      f. **Coltsfoot**
    g. **Gorse**
14. **The Snowdrop**
    It hangs its head to protect the pollen from rain and snow.
15. **Brimstone**
16. a. **Hares** are bigger than **rabbits** and have longer ears with black tips on them.
17. **A Vixen**
18. **A Doe Rabbit**
19. **A Buck Rabbit**
20. **Fox and Cub**          **Horse and Foal**
    **Hare and Leveret**    **Goat and Kid**
    **Sheep and Lamb**      **Deer and Fawn**
    **Cow and Calf**
21. **A Fox lives in an Earth**
    **A Rabbit lives in a Burrow**
    **A Squirrel lives in a Drey**
    **A Badger lives in a Set**
22. b. **Stoats** are bigger than **weasels** and have black-tipped tails.
23. **The Stickleback**
24. **Frogspawn**
25. a. **Sowing barley and oats**
    g. **Sowing potatoes and sugar beet**

**Answer to the Question on page 12**
The thirteenth century began in the year 1200 and ended in 1299. (Some people argue that a century does not begin until a year later, so that they would say the thirteenth century began in 1201 and ended in 1300.)

# SUMMER

We all love Summer when the days are long and the nights so often bright with stars. In Britain we are lucky because wherever we live we are not so very far from the sea. But before we reach the restless waves we travel through the countryside and that is more exciting with the help of this book. If you stop for a picnic—and be sure to take your litter with you when you leave—'Be still, look and listen' is a good rule when in the country. I have never been able to resist exploring a wood. I love to hear the whisper of the wind in the tree tops and, when I was your age I used to keep a notebook and record the place, date and list of trees and woodland flowers I could recognise. I should have been quicker and more accurate if I had used this book. There are some birds you are more likely to see and hear in the shelter of a wood than outside. And there are many flowers, which prefer the shade of the woodland. **Bluebells** for instance and the frail **Wood Anemones** in early Summer. Down the lanes in summertime, where the hedges are high, you may smell **Honeysuckle** before you see it, but the dainty pink **Wild Rose**, which blooms profusely in June does not seem to smell. But **Meadowsweet** does and that you will find near water.

So much to see, enjoy and to remember out of doors in a British Summer. As dusk falls at the end of a long day the baby rabbits come out to play. Perhaps you may see a fox slipping silently, like a dusky shadow, along the hedgerow, looking for his supper. But Summer is too short. July marks the turn of the year and August is the month of harvest.

Make the most of Summer.

# A Boy's Song

*Where the pools are bright and deep,*
*Where the grey trout lies asleep,*
*Up the river and over the lea,*
*That's the way for Billy and me.*

*Where the blackbird sings the latest,*
*Where the hawthorn blooms the sweetest,*
*Where the nestlings chirp and flee,*
*That's the way for Billy and me.*

*Where the mowers mow the cleanest,*
*Where the hay lies thick and greenest,*
*There to track the homeward bee,*
*That's the way for Billy and me.*

*Where the hazel bank is steepest,*
*Where the shadow falls the deepest,*
*Where the clustering nuts fall free,*
*That's the way for Billy and me.*

*Why the boys should drive away*
*Little sweet maidens from the play,*
*Or love to banter and fight so well,*
*That's the thing I never could tell.*

*But this I know, I love to play*
*Through the meadow, among the hay;*
*Up the water and over the lea,*
*That's the way for Billy and me.*

**James Hogg**

# SUMMER QUIZ

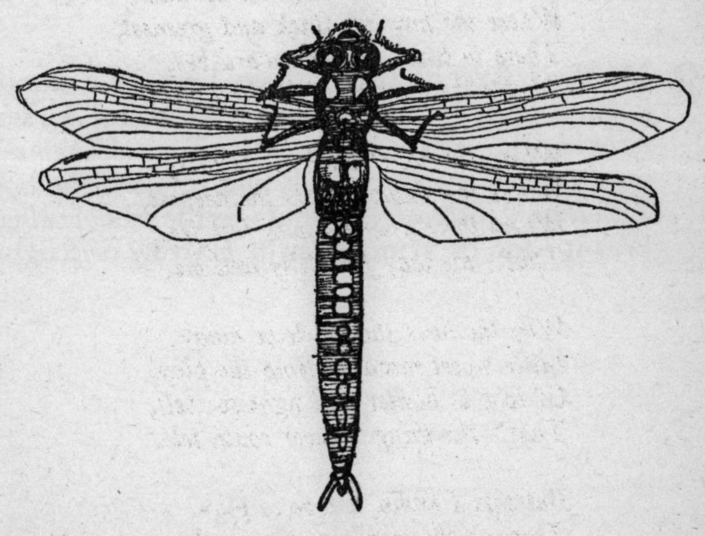

# The High Midsummer

*Soon will the high Midsummer pomps come on,*
*Soon will the musk carnations break and swell,*
*Soon shall we have gold-dusted snapdragon,*
*Sweet-William with his homely cottage-smell*
*And stocks in fragrant blow.*

**Q.** Matthew Arnold wrote those lines in a famous poem called 'Thyrsis'. He was the son of Thomas Arnold, who was the headmaster of one of England's most famous public schools and inspired the book *Tom Brown's Schooldays*. What was the school called? Was it Eton or Winchester or Harrow or Rugby?

**1.** Here are the names of thirteen trees:

> **Hawthorn**
> **Cherry**
> **Holly**
> **Mountain Ash**
> **Fir**
> **Yew**
> **Hornbeam**
> **Beech**
> **Crab Apple**
> **Cypress**
> **Pine**
> **Elm**
> **Chestnut**

Six of the trees are ones you would find in bloom in early Summer. Can you spot the names of the six?

You will find the six trees illustrated on the next page. Can you put the correct name to each drawing?

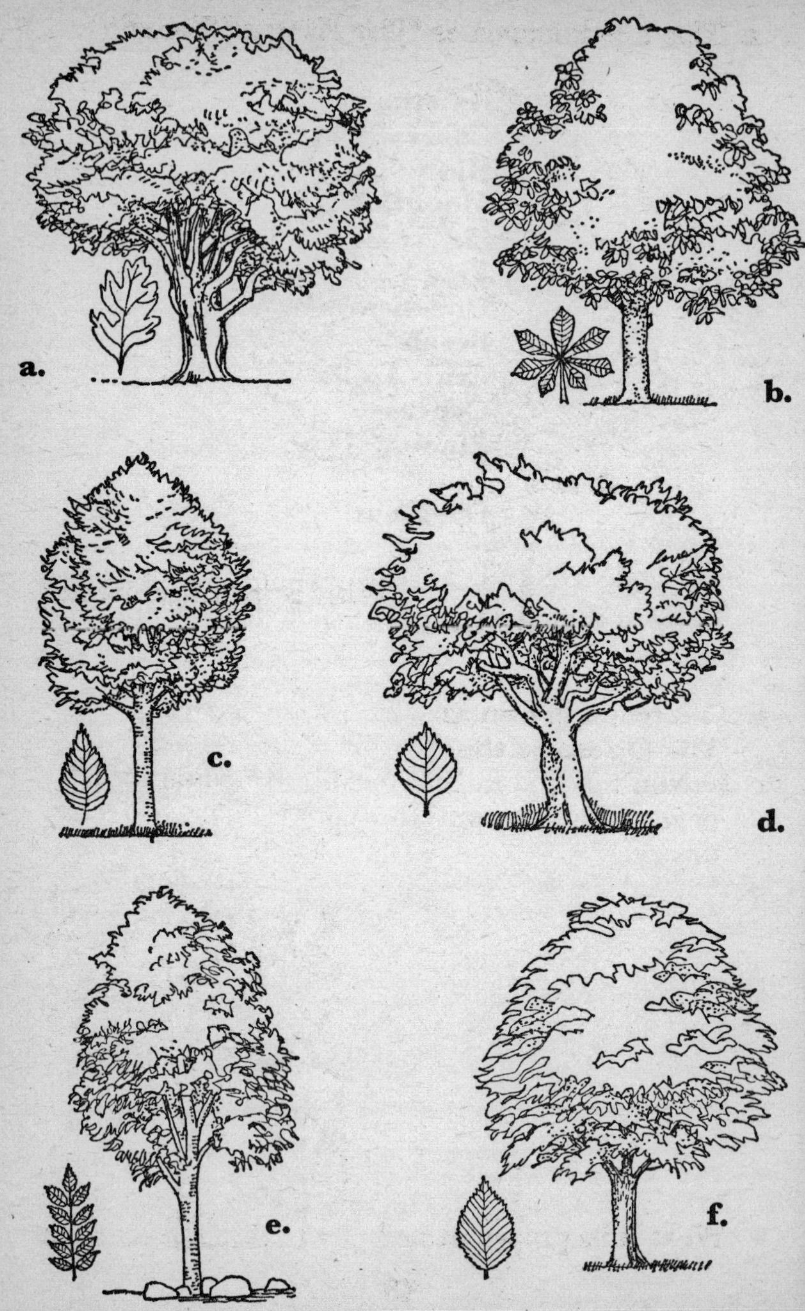

**2.** This tree is known as **'The King of Trees'**:

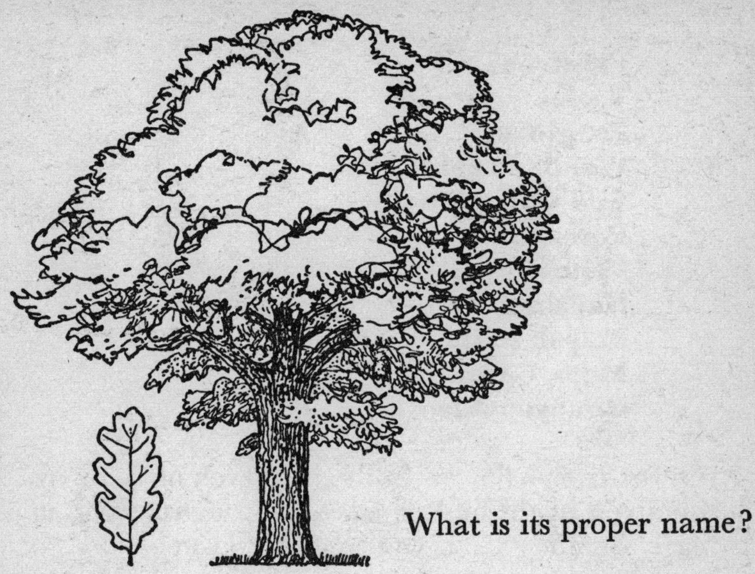

What is its proper name?

**3.** This tree is known as **'The Queen of the Forest'**:

What is its proper name?

**4.** Here is a list of twelve flowers:

> **Wood Anemone**
> **Primrose**
> **Violet**
> **Foxglove**
> **Wood Sorrel**
> **Red Campion**
> **Poppy**
> **Yellow Flag**
> **Harebell**
> **Marsh Marigold (or Kingcup)**
> **Moss Campion**
> **Honeysuckle**

Of the twelve flowers in the list, seven of them are ones you might find on a walk through a wood in early Summer. Can you spot the seven?

You will find all seven flowers illustrated below and on the next page. Can you give each flower its proper name?

a. 

 b.

c.

d.

e.

f.

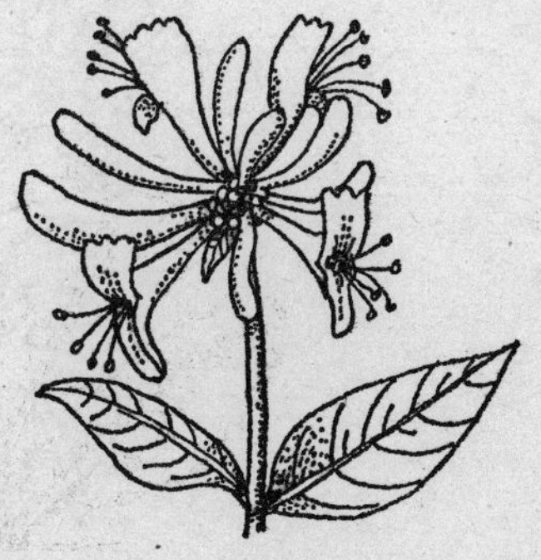

g.

45

**5.** Here are six different flowers that you might find growing near ponds and ditches in the Summer:

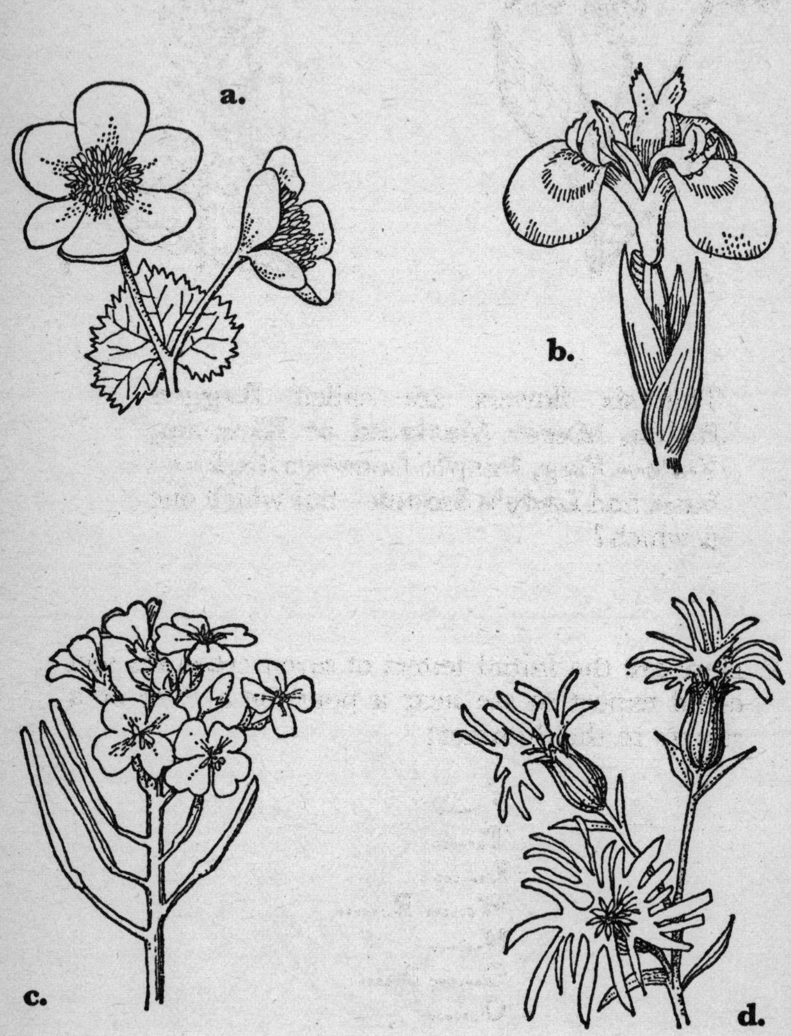

e.

f.

The six flowers are called **Ragged Robin, Marsh Marigold or Kingcup, Yellow Flag, Purple Loosestrife, Fleabane** and **Lady's Smock**—but which one is which?

**6.** Here are the initial letters of seven creatures you could expect to see near a pond or a river or a stream in the Summer:

F......
T.......
L......
W....... R......
N......
G...... S......
O......

Can you give the full names of the seven creatures?

 Here are six of the birds you could see near a
pond, river or stream in the Summer:

f.

Can you name them?

**8.** These birds all belong to one family:

> **Yellow Bunting**
> **Corn Bunting**
> **Reed Bunting**
> **Hawfinch**
> **Goldfinch**
> **Chaffinch**
> **Greenfinch**
> **Bullfinch**
> **Yellow-Hammer**
> **Linnet**

What is the 'family' called?

**9.** What bird with a long tail and wings, slate-grey plumage with white underparts barred with dark grey, has a very distinctive call that you can hear in early Summer?

**10.** A famous owl has a call which goes: '*Tu-whit, Tu-hoo*'. What is the owl's proper name?

**11.** Can you name an animal that can fly?

**12.** One of these creatures is a **Frog** and one is a **Toad**:

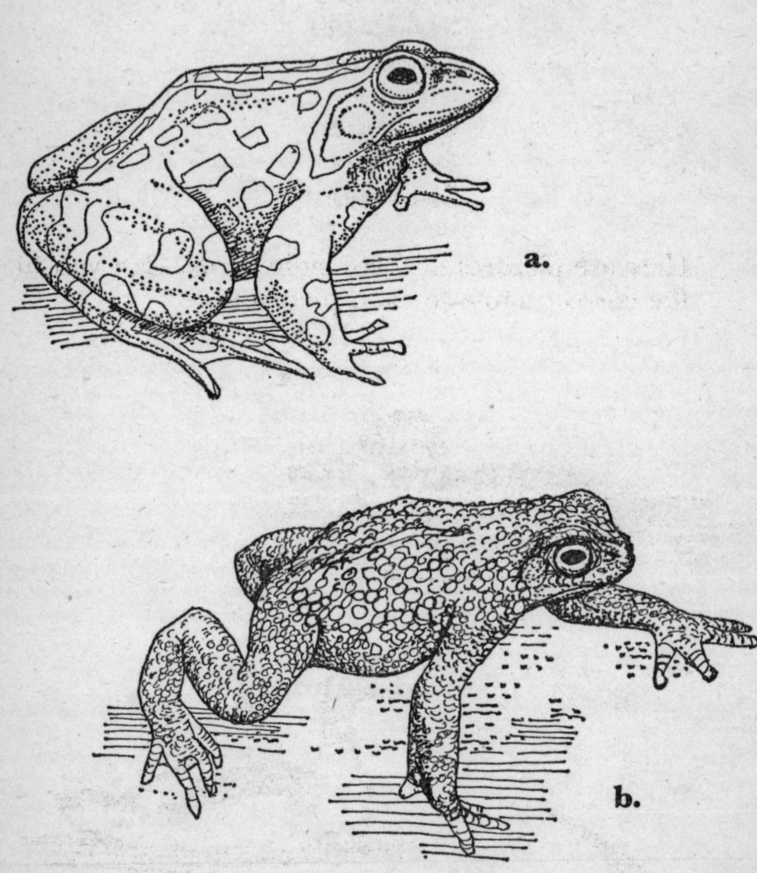


But which is the **Frog** and which is the **Toad**?

**13.** In the Summer you can see all sorts of birds whose names begin with the letter S, such as these:

> **Shrike**
> **Spoonbill**
> **Sandpiper**
> **Stonechat**
> **Swift**
> **Shelduck**
> **Swallow**
> **Shoveler**

Here are pictures of these eight birds. Can you fit the correct name to each picture?

a.

b.

c.

d.
e.
f.
g.
h.

**14.** Of these wild flowers, how many are red or pink?

> **Sorrel**
> **Bramble**
> **Sweet Briar**
> **Dog Rose**
> **Red Deadnettle**
> **Poppy**
> **Scarlet Pimpernel**
> **Bindweed**
> **Foxglove**
> **Red Campion**
> **Dove's-Foot**
> **Crane's-Bill**
> **Red Clover**
> **Rest-Harrow**
> **Ragged Robin**
> **Willow Herb**
> **Corn Cockle**
> **Spur Valerium**

**15.** What is the name of the insect you can see in the Summer which makes a chirruping sound, and hops?

**16.** These five birds usually leave the British Isles before the Summer ends:

**d.**

**e.**

What are the five birds called?

**17.** Of these six birds, three can be heard at night:

> **Nightingales**
> **Skylarks**
> **Warblers**
> **Rooks**
> **Owls**
> **Nightjars**

Which three?

**18.** **a.** This owl nests in barns, towers, ruins, woods and farm buildings:

What is it called?

**b.** This owl lives mainly in fields and hedges:

What is it called?

**c.** This owl lives in the open country:

What is it called?

**d.** This owl lives in woods, especially in fir trees:

What is it called?

**e.** This owl lives mainly in woods, parks and large gardens:

What is it called?

**19.** Here is a list of the names of twenty butterflies:

**Large White**
**Small White**
**Brimstone**
**Red Admiral**
**Large Tortoiseshell**
**Small Tortoiseshell**
**Peacock**
**Painted Lady**
**Small Copper**
**Meadow Brown**
**Common Blue**
**Purple Emperor**
**Dark Green Fritillary**
**Adonis Blue**
**Privet Hawkmoth**
**Leaf Butterfly**
**Black-veined White**
**Magpie**
**Kentish Glory**
**Rice Paper**

Eleven of them are butterflies that you could easily find in the British Isles in the Summer. Can you spot the eleven?

**20.** Here are eight of the insects you might see in the
Summer:

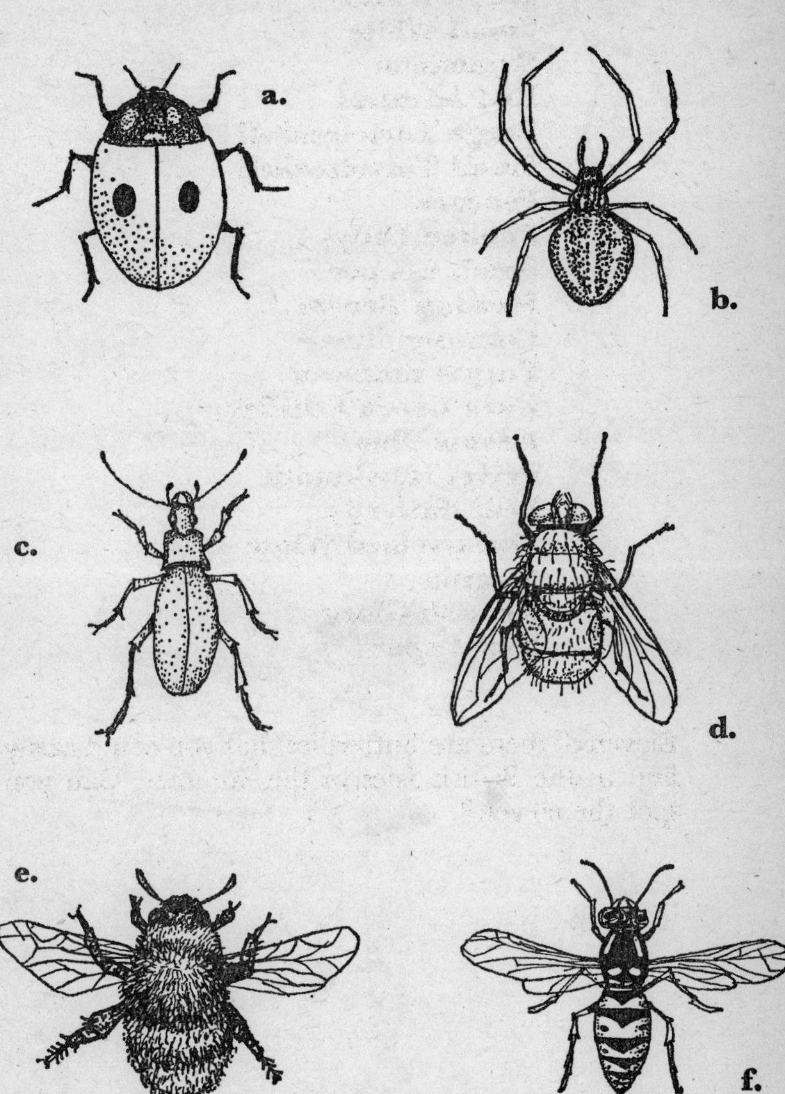

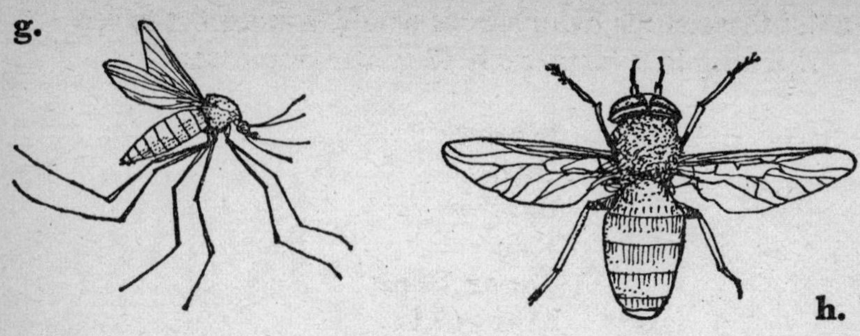

Can you name them?

21. This is a brightly-coloured winged insect you often find near water:

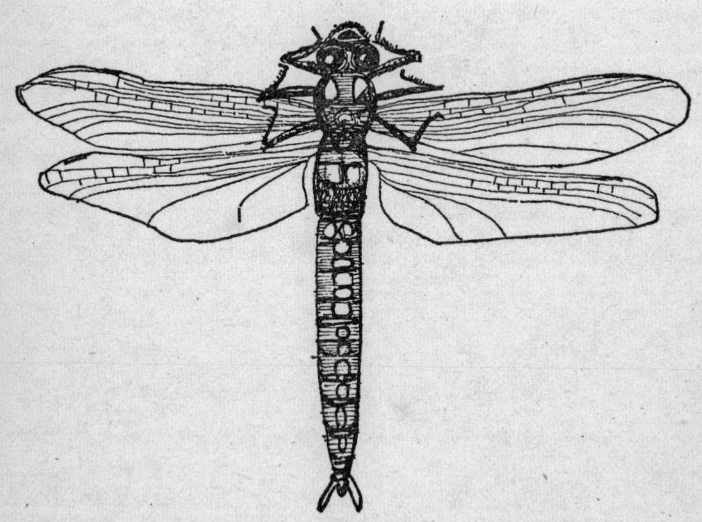

What is it called?

**22.** Of these crops, which ones would you expect to see ripening in a farmer's field in the Summer:

> **Wheat**
> **Oats**
> **Barley**
> **Rye**
> **Sugar Beet**
> **Mangolds**
> **Swedes**
> **Potatoes**

**23.** Of these animals, birds and insects, which ones are regarded as pests and the farmer's enemies:

> **Rabbits**
> **Snails**
> **Grey Squirrels**
> **Caterpillars**
> **Rats**
> **Foxes**
> **Pigeons**
> **Slugs**

**24.** Of the animals and insects in this list which ones
come out at night:

> **Bats**
> **Hedgehogs**
> **Badgers**
> **Otters**
> **Glow-worms**
> **Dormice**
> **Moths**
> **Voles**
> **Moles**
> **Foxes**
> **Hares**

**25.** One of these animals hides in cornfields during
harvesting:

> **Badger**
> **Stoat**
> **Weasel**
> **Rabbit**
> **Squirrel**
> **Fox**
> **Otter**
> **Cow**
> **Ferret**

Which one?

# What Is Pink?

*What is pink? A rose is pink*
*By the fountain's brink.*
*What is red? A poppy's red*
*In its barley bed.*
*What is blue? The sky is blue*
*Where the clouds float through.*
*What is white? A swan is white*
*Sailing in the light.*
*What is yellow? Pears are yellow*
*Rich and ripe and mellow.*
*What is green? The grass is green*
*With small flowers between.*
*What is violet? Clouds are violet*
*In the summer twilight.*
*What is orange? Why, an orange,*
*Just an orange!*

**Christina Rossetti**

# Answers to the Summer Quiz

1. a. Hawthorn      b. Chestnut
   c. Cherry      d. Crab Apple
   e. Mountain Ash      f. Hornbeam
2. Oak
3. Silver Birch
4. a. Wood Anemone      b. Primrose
   c. Violet      d. Foxglove
   e. Wood Sorrel      f. Red Campion
   g. Honeysuckle
5. a. Marsh Marigold (or Kingcup)
   b. Yellow Flag      c. Lady's Smock
   d. Ragged Robin      e. Fleabane
   f. Purple Loosestrife
6. Frog      Water Rat
   Toad      Newt
   Lizard      Grass Snake
   Otter
7. a. Kingfisher      b. Moorhen
   c. Coot      d. Swan
   e. Duck      f. Heron
8. All the birds in the list belong to the **Finch** family.
9. Cuckoo
10. **Tawny Owl,** also known as **Wood Owl**
11. **Bat**
12. **a.** is the **Frog** and **b.** is the **Toad.** Toads waddle and are shorter and thicker than frogs, with warts covering their backs. They are also darker than frogs and not such keen swimmers.
13. a. Shoveler      b. Shelduck
    c. Swift      d. Swallow
    e. Stonechat      f. Spoonbill
    g. Shrike      h. Sandpiper

14. All of them are either red or pink.
15. **The Grasshopper**
16. **a. Swallow**      **b. Cuckoo**
    **c. Swift**      **d. Sand Martin**
    **e. House Martin**
17. **Nightingales, Owls, Nightjars**
18. **a. Barn Owl**      **b. Little Owl**
    **c. Short-eared Owl**      **d. Long-eared Owl**
    **e. Tawny (or Wood) Owl**
19. **Large White**      **Peacock**
    **Small White**      **Painted Lady**
    **Brimstone**      **Small Copper**
    **Red Admiral**      **Meadow Brown**
    **Large Tortoiseshell**      **Common Blue**
    **Small Tortoiseshell**
20. **a. Ladybird**      **b. Spider**
    **c. Beetle**      **d. House-fly**
    **e. Bumble-bee**      **f. Wasp**
    **g. Mosquito**      **h. Horse-fly**
21. **The Dragonfly**
22. All of them.
23. All of them.
24. **Bats, Hedgehogs, Badgers, Otters, Glow-worms, Dormice, Moths**
25. **Rabbit**

**Answer to the Question on page 40**
Rugby.

# AUTUMN

September is a month of ripeness and gorgeous colours. The farmer brings his harvest home, the swallows who came to us in May leave us, and the summer flies with them. There is harvest for you too in the hedgerows—juicy **Blackberries** and crisp **Hazel Nuts**. And in some fields, if you get up early enough, you may find **Mushrooms**—but be sure that they are mushrooms and not poisonous fungi.

In the woods the **Squirrels** are busy gathering their harvest of acorns and the tiny, triangular nuts that fall from the rough husks of the Beech trees. These tasty nuts are called **Beech-mast**.

Not so many wild flowers now, but down the hedgerows you may see the white tufts of **Traveller's Joy** like a snowy plumage. You will soon see why another name for this plant is **Old Man's Beard**, and it is the seeds of **Wild Clematis**.

After the harvest is in the farmer ploughs his fields. You may hear the throb of his tractors before you see a cloud of birds following and settling on the straight furrows.

Spring is green with growth, but October is golden with fruitfulness. The **Bracken** in the hedgerows is brown. **Holly berries** are changing colour and leaves of **Beech** and **Oak** are turning gold. Not so much bird song now. October often brings rain and the woods, with their carpet of fallen leaves, smell of sweet decay. In sheltered places you may still find a few woodland flowers. The year is dying with dignity and beauty and the countryside is ready, like the Hedgehog, for its winter sleep.

# Autumn

*I love the fitful gust that shakes*
   *The casement all the day,*
*And from the glossy elm tree takes*
   *The faded leaves away,*
*Twirling them by the window-pane*
*With thousand others down the lane.*

*I love to see the shaking twig*
   *Dance till shut of eve,*
*The sparrow on the cottage rig,*
   *Whose chirp would make believe*
*That Spring was just now flirting by*
*In Summer's lap with flowers to lie.*

*I love to see the cottage smoke*
   *Curl upwards through the trees;*
*The pigeons nestled round the cote*
   *On November days like these;*
*The cock upon the dunghill crowing,*
*The mill sails on the heath a-going.*

**John Clare**

# AUTUMN QUIZ

# To Autumn

*Season of mists and mellow fruitfulness!*
  *Close bosom-friend of the maturing sun;*
*Conspiring with him how to load and bless*
  *With fruit the vines that round the thatch-eaves run;*
*To bend with apples the moss'd cottage-trees,*
  *And fill all fruit with ripeness to the core;*
    *To swell the gourd, and plump the hazel shells*
*With a sweet kernel; to set budding more,*
*And still more, later flowers for the bees,*
*Until they think warm days will never cease,*
  *For Summer has o'er-brimmed their clammy cells.*

**Q.** This is the first verse of one of the greatest poems in the English language written by one of England's greatest poets. He was born in 1795 and died when he was only twenty-six years old. What was his name? Was it John Keats or William Wordsworth or William Shakespeare?

**1.** These are all fruits you will find growing in the Autumn:

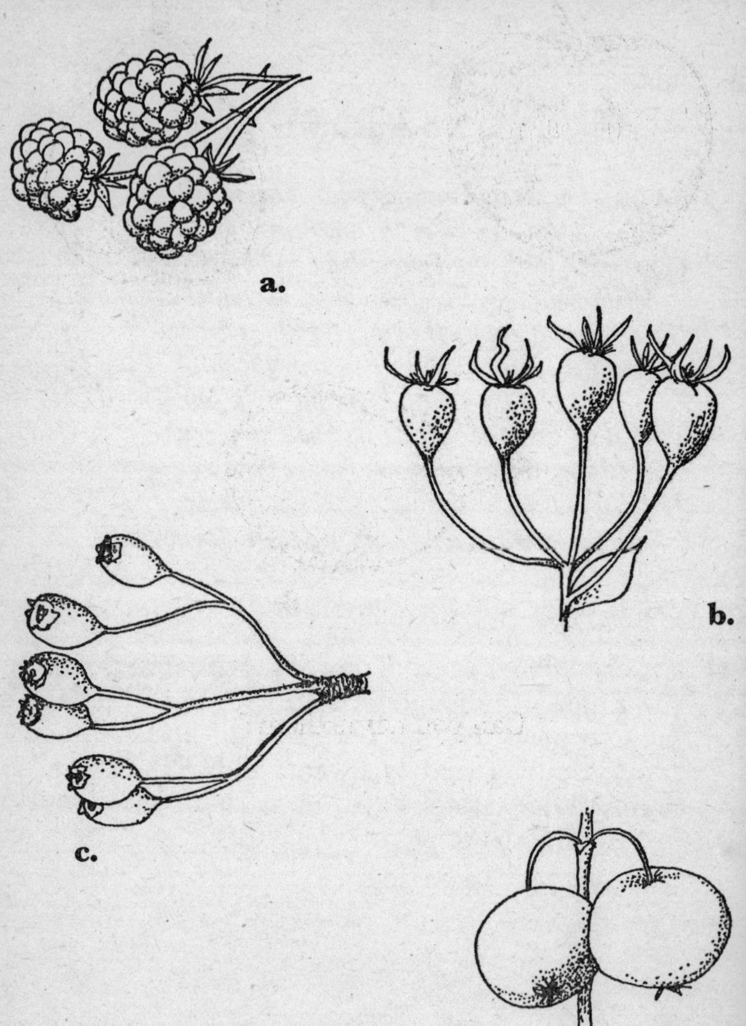

a.

b.

c.

d.

e.

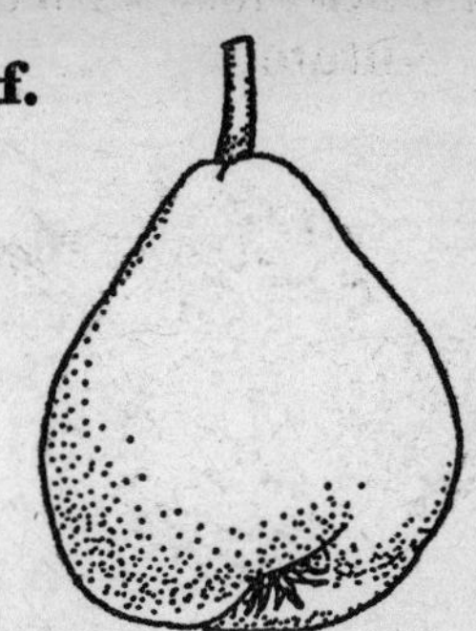

f.

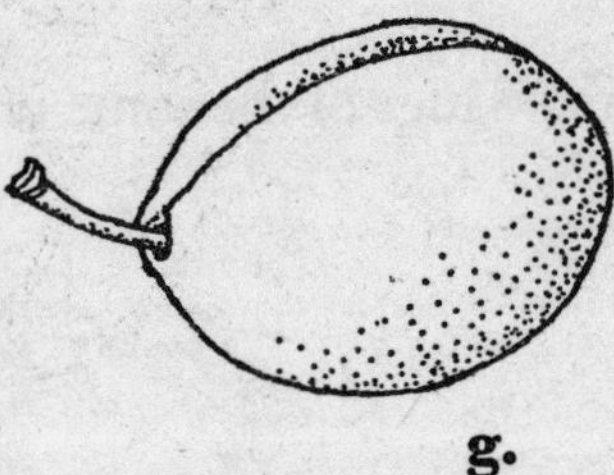

g.

Can you name them?

**2.** Here are the names of ten wild flowers which you can still find in Britain in the Autumn:

**Buttercup**
**Ragwort**
**Red Clover**
**Deadnettle**
**Thistle**
**Scarlet Pimpernel**
**Water Mint**
**Toad Flax**
**White Campion**
**Wild Pansy**

And here are drawings of the same wild flowers:

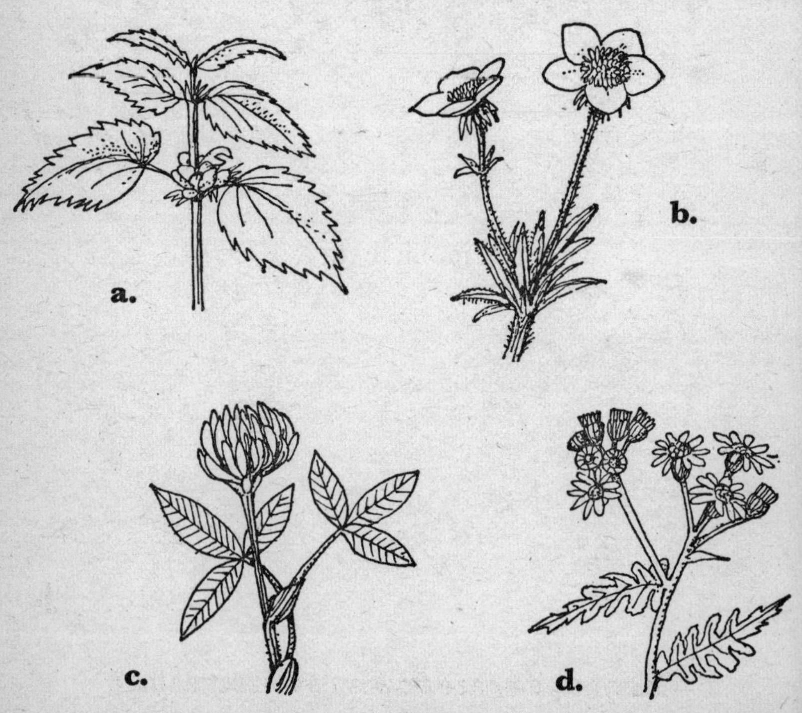

a.

b.

c.

d.

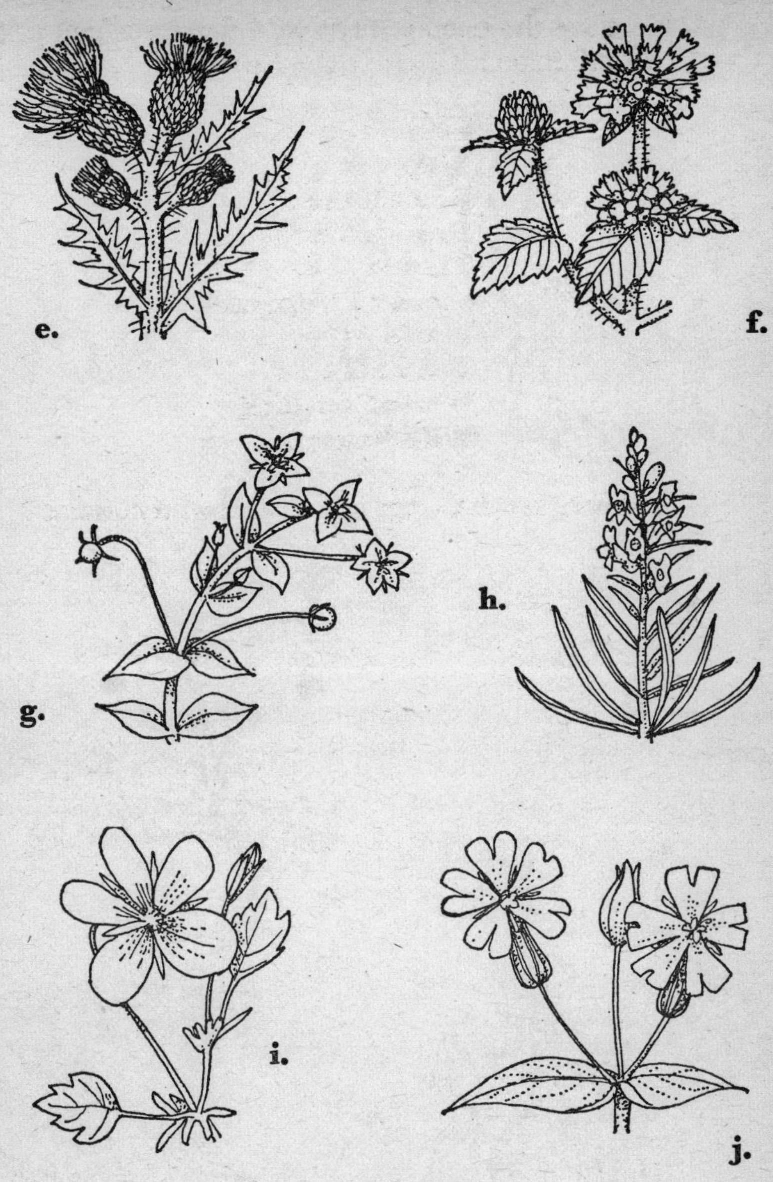

Can you give each flower its correct name?

**3.** These three types of deer can be found in Britain in the Autumn:

What is each deer called?

**4.** What are deers' horns called?

**5.** One of these animals sometimes takes over part of a
rabbit warren as his own home:

**Badger**
**Fox**
**Stoat**
**Weasel**
**Vole**
**Mole**
**Dormouse**
**Squirrel**

Which one?

**6.** There is a pair of animals that will sometimes share
a home together. It is one of these pairs:

**Weasel and Stoat**
**Squirrel and Fieldmouse**
**Fox and Badger**
**Vole and Mole**
**Lamb and Wolf**

Do you know which pair it is?

**7.** What is the name of this large black-and-white bird with a long tail:

**8.** What is the name of this little animal that is so feared by rabbits:

**9.** Here are four of the nuts you can see in the
Autumn:

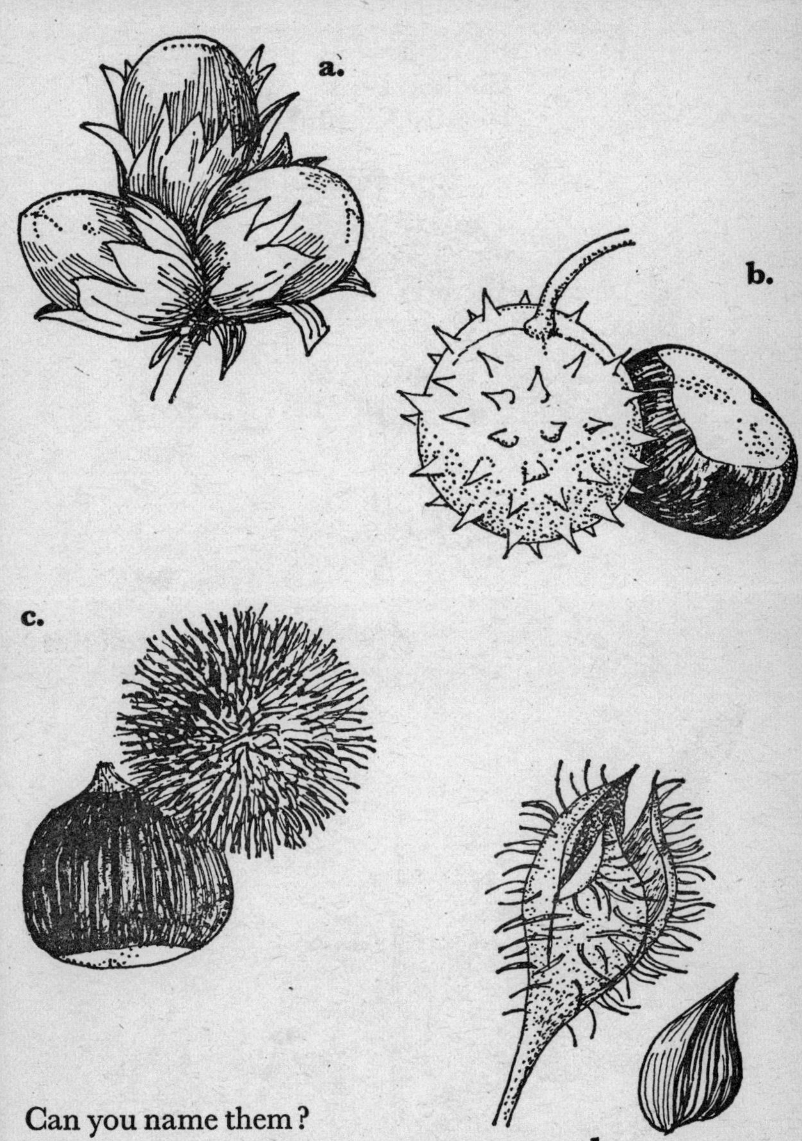

Can you name them?

**10.** Here are the names of six poisonous fruits and
flowers:

> **Black Bryony**
> **Cuckoo Pint**
> **Deadly Nightshade**
> **Yew**
> **Spindle Tree**
> **Thorn Apple**

And here are pictures of the same six fruits and
flowers:

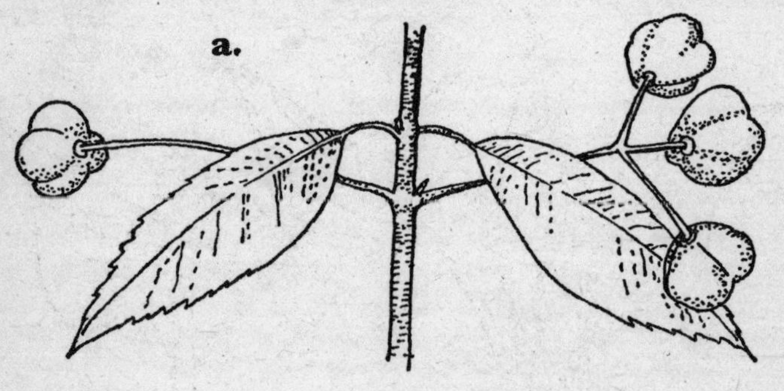


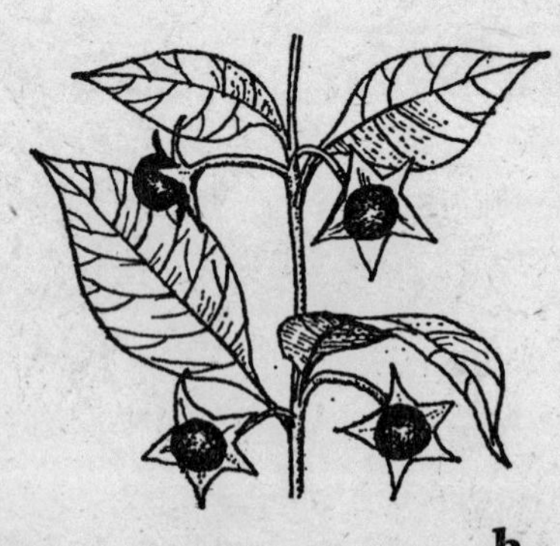

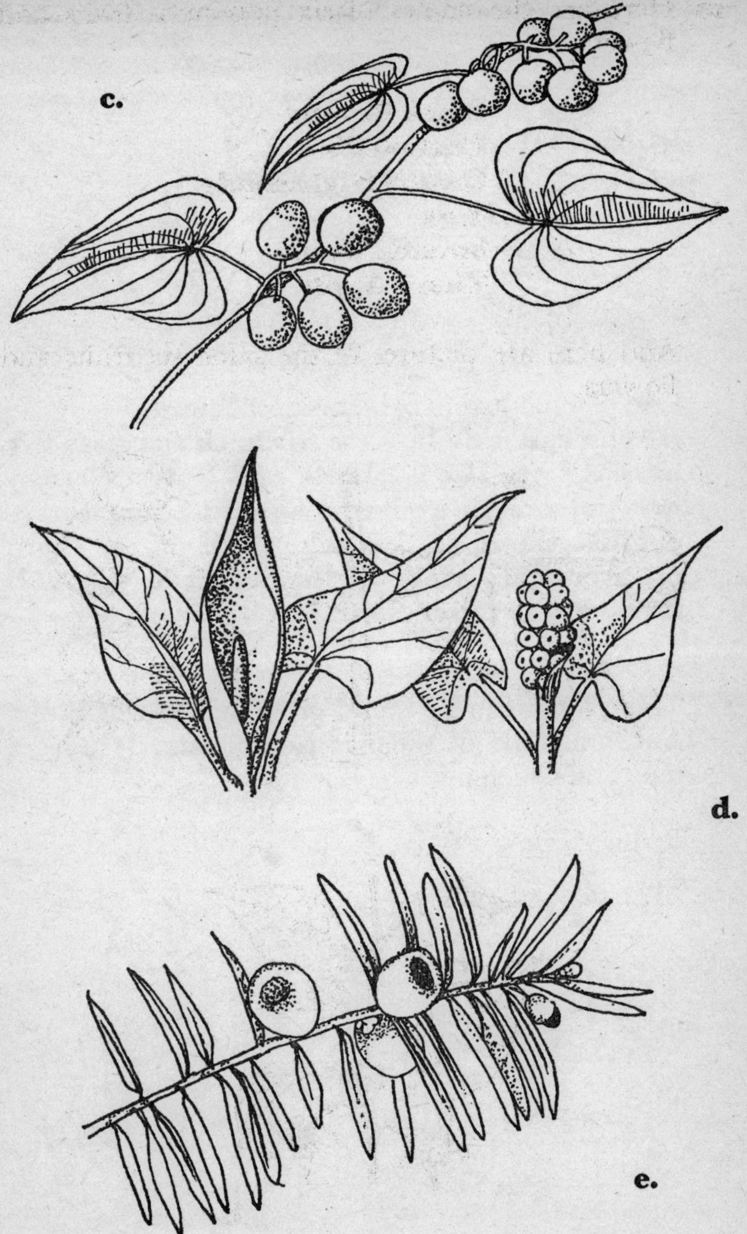


c.

d.

e.

f.

Can you name the six plants and flowers?
**(If you can't, do be sure to check the answers on page 93. These plants and flowers really are poisonous and you should learn to recognise them, so that when you do see them on a country walk in the Autumn you will know not to touch them.)**

**11.** These fungi can be found growing in fields in the Autumn. One of them is **poisonous**. What are they and which one is poisonous?

a.

b.

c.

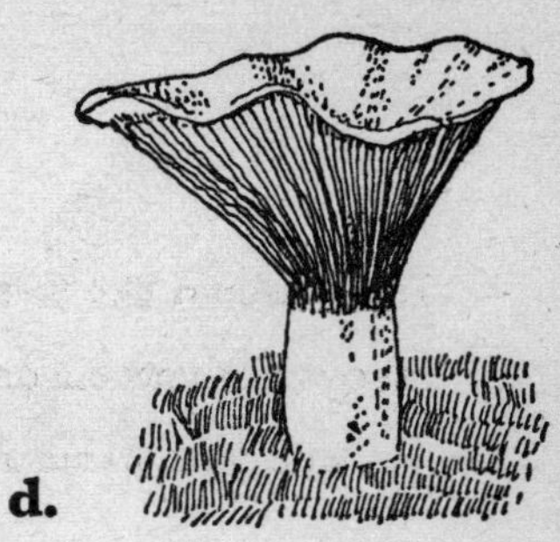

d.

**12.** Of these fifteen birds, five will be leaving the British Isles in the Autumn:

> **Swallows**
> **Martins**
> **Blue Tits**
> **Robins**
> **Bullfinches**
> **Warblers**
> **Cranes**
> **Dippers**
> **Chiff-Chaffs**
> **Woodpeckers**
> **Starlings**
> **Shrikes**
> **Cuckoos**
> **Sparrows**
> **Thrushes**

Can you spot the five?

**13.** This is the most common bird in the British Isles:

What is it called?

**14.** This is a bird that you can sometimes see flying over and settling on a farmer's fields in the Autumn:

What is it called? And why is it rather surprising to find this bird flying over farmland?

**15.** What are the names of each of these birds:

**16.** Here are the names of five birds that come over to the British Isles from overseas in the Autumn:

> **Fieldfares**
> **Bramblings**
> **Snow Buntings**
> **Brent Geese**
> **Pinkfooted Geese**

And here are drawings of all five birds:

Can you give the right name to each bird?

**17.** Here are the two birds of prey that you are most likely to see in the British Isles:

What are they called?

**18.** In this building hops are dried:

What is the building called?

Is it:

        **a.** **A Granary?**
        **b.** **A Dutch Barn?**
        **c.** **A Windmill?**
        **d.** **A Hop House?**
        **e.** **A Lighthouse?**
        **f.** **An Oasthouse?**
        **g.** **A Hopscotch House?**

**19.** What is the field in which hops are grown called?

Is it:

> **A Hop Field?**
> **A Hop Garden?**
> **A Hop Harvest?**
> **A Hop Yard?**
> **A Hop Orchard?**
> **A Hop Terrace?**
> **A Hop Acre?**
> **A Hopelot?**
> **A Hop Forest?**
> **A Hop Earth?**
> **A Hop O' My Thumb?**

And what are hops used for?

Are they used for:

> **Making Instant Mashed Potato?**
> **Making roofs for thatched cottages?**
> **Making glue?**
> **Making beer?**
> **Making soap and perfume?**
> **Making string and twine?**
> **Making Coca-Cola?**
> **Making turpentine?**
> **Making honey?**
> **Making stubble?**
> **Making manure?**

**20.** This is a bird that lays eggs nearly all the year round:

What is it called?

And what colour are its eggs?

Are they:

        **a. White?**
        **b. Light blue?**
        **c. Speckled brown?**
        **d. Speckled yellow?**
        **e. Light green?**
        **f. Light brown?**

**21.** What is a **deciduous** tree?

Is it:
a. **A tree that sheds its leaves in the Autumn?**
b. **A tree that is evergreen?**
c. **A tree that sheds its leaves in the Spring?**
d. **A tree suffering from Dutch Elm disease?**
e. **A tree that sheds its leaves in the Summer?**
f. **A tree that bears edible fruit?**
g. **A tropical tree that does not grow in Europe?**
h. **A South American tree unknown in the Northern hemisphere?**

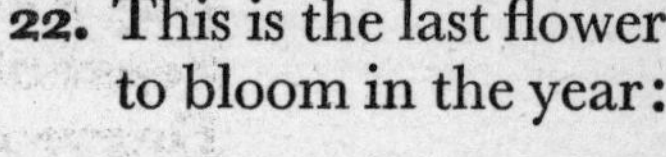

**22.** This is the last flower to bloom in the year:

What is it called?

**23.** Two of the animals in this list are busy in the
Autumn eating as many nuts as they can find and
storing them away for the winter months:

> **Squirrel**
> **Weasel**
> **Mole**
> **Dormouse**
> **Hamster**
> **Hedgehog**
> **Stoat**
> **Ferret**

Can you spot the two?

**24.** What is the Festival held in early Autumn that is
closely connected with country life and farming?

Is it:

> **Hallowe'en?**
> **Guy Fawkes' Night?**
> **Feast of Saint Nicholas?**
> **Harvest Festival?**
> **Michaelmas?**
> **Festival of Candles?**
> **May Day?**

**25.** Which of these jobs would you expect to see a farmer doing during the Autumn?

**Potato picking**
**Hop picking**
**Harvesting sugar beet**
**Harvesting mangolds**
**Harvesting turnips**
**Harvesting swedes**
**Ploughing fields**
**Sowing wheat**

*In the other gardens*
*And all up the vale,*
*From the autumn bonfires*
*See the smoke trail!*

*Pleasant summer over*
*And all the summer flowers,*
*The red fire blazes,*
*The grey smoke towers.*

*Sing a song of seasons!*
*Something bright in all!*
*Flowers in the summer,*
*Fires in the fall!*

**Robert Louis Stevenson**

# Answers to the Autumn Quiz

1.  a. Blackberries     b. Hips
    c. Haws     d. Crab Apples
    e. Apples     f.  Pears
    g. Plums
2.  a. Deadnettle     b. Buttercup
    c. Red Clover     d. Ragwort
    e. Thistle     f. Water Mint
    g. Scarlet Pimpernel     h. Toad Flax
    i. Wild Pansy     j. White Campion
3.  a. Roe Deer
    b. Red Deer
    c. Fallow Deer
4.  Antlers
5.  The Badger
6.  The Fox and the Badger
7.  Magpie
8.  Stoat
9.  a. Hazel     b. Horse-Chestnut
    c. Sweet Chestnut     d. Beech
10. a. Spindle-Tree     b. Deadly Nightshade
    c. Black Briony     d. Cuckoo Pint
    e. Yew     f. Thorn Apple
11. a. Death Cap     b. Shaggy Ink Cup
    c. Puff Ball     d. Chanterelle
    The Death Cap is poisonous.
12. Swallows     Chiff-Chaffs
    Martins     Warblers
    Cuckoos
13. Blackbird

14.    **A Gull.** It is surprising to see gulls flying over farmland because they are sea birds, but they like to gobble up the grubs and worms thrown up by the farmer's plough.

15.    a. **Partridge**          b. **Grouse**
       c. **Woodcock**          d. **Pheasant**
16.    a. **Pinkfooted Geese**  b. **Fieldfares**
       c. **Brent Geese**       d. **Bramblings**
       e. **Snow Buntings**
17.    a. **Sparrow Hawk**      b. **Kestrel**
18.    **An Oasthouse**
19.    **A Hop Garden**
       Making Beer
20.    **Wood Pigeon**
       White
21.    **A tree that sheds its leaves in the Autumn**
22.    **Ivy**
23.    **Squirrel and Dormouse**
24.    **Harvest Festival**
25.    **All of them!**

**Answer to the Question on page 69**
John Keats.

# WINTER

December often brings snow and frost. As the days shorten and we plan for Christmas, there does not seem much time for expeditions to the countryside, unless we are in search of holly berries! This is a pity because nature still has much to show us. If there is snow it is interesting to study the tracks of birds and such animals as **Rabbits**, **Stoats** and **Foxes**. **Hips** (the red seeds of the Wild Rose) and **Haws** (the scarlet berries of the Hawthorn trees, which gave us such sweet-scented pleasure in May) still blaze in the hedges.

Did you know that the **Robin** and the **Song Thrush** sing just as freely and sweetly this month as they did in August? Indeed these two friends cheer us through the dark days and share their joy with us when Spring comes again.

And now that the leaves have fallen from so many woodland trees, it is easier to recognise those we call **'Evergreens'** because they do not shed their leaves in Autumn. More about these on page 98.

Some animals go to sleep through the Winter, which seems rather sensible. The **Hedgehog** does this under a hedge or in a ditch and the little **Dormouse** is another animal, which goes into what we call 'hibernation', but you will not find him because his bedroom is underground. He covers the entrance with grass and foliage and goes to sleep surrounded by nuts and haws to eat when he wakes.

But the most wonderful thing about winter—another miracle—is that it cannot stay for ever. The country-side is only resting ready to be born again in Spring.

# Winter

*Sweet blackbird is silenced with chaffinch and thrush,*
*Only waistcoated robin still chirps in the bush:*
*Soft sun-loving swallows have mustered in force,*
*And winged in the spice-teeming southlands their course.*

*Plump housekeeper dormouse has tucked himself neat,*
*Just a brown ball in moss with a morsel to eat:*
*Armed hedgehog has huddled him into the hedge,*
*While frogs scarce miss freezing deep down in the sedge.*

*Soft swallows have left us alone in the lurch,*
*But robin sits whistling to us from his perch:*
*If I were red robin, I'd pipe you a tune,*
*Would make you despise all the beauties of June.*

*But, since that cannot be, let us draw round the fire,*
*Munch chestnuts, tell stories, and stir the blaze higher:*
*We'll comfort pinched robin with crumbs, little man,*
*Till he'll sing us the very best song that he can.*

**Christina Rossetti**

# WINTER QUIZ

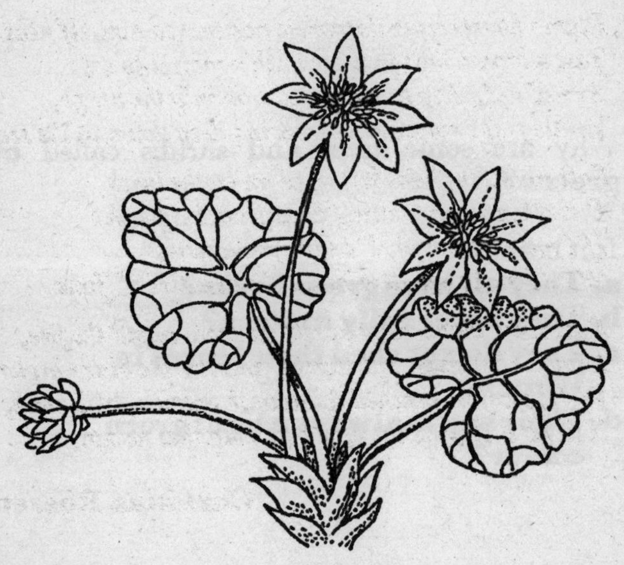

# A Winter Riddle

*In Spring I look gay*
*Decked in comely array;*
*In Summer more clothing I wear;*
*When colder it grows,*
*I fling off my clothes;*
*And in Winter quite naked appear!*

**Q.** What am I?

**1.** Why are some trees and shrubs called **evergreens?**

Is it because:
a. **They all have green barks?**
b. **They never fully mature?**
c. **They do not shed their leaves in Winter?**
d. **Their sap is always a light green colour?**

**2.** Here are drawings of six evergreens:

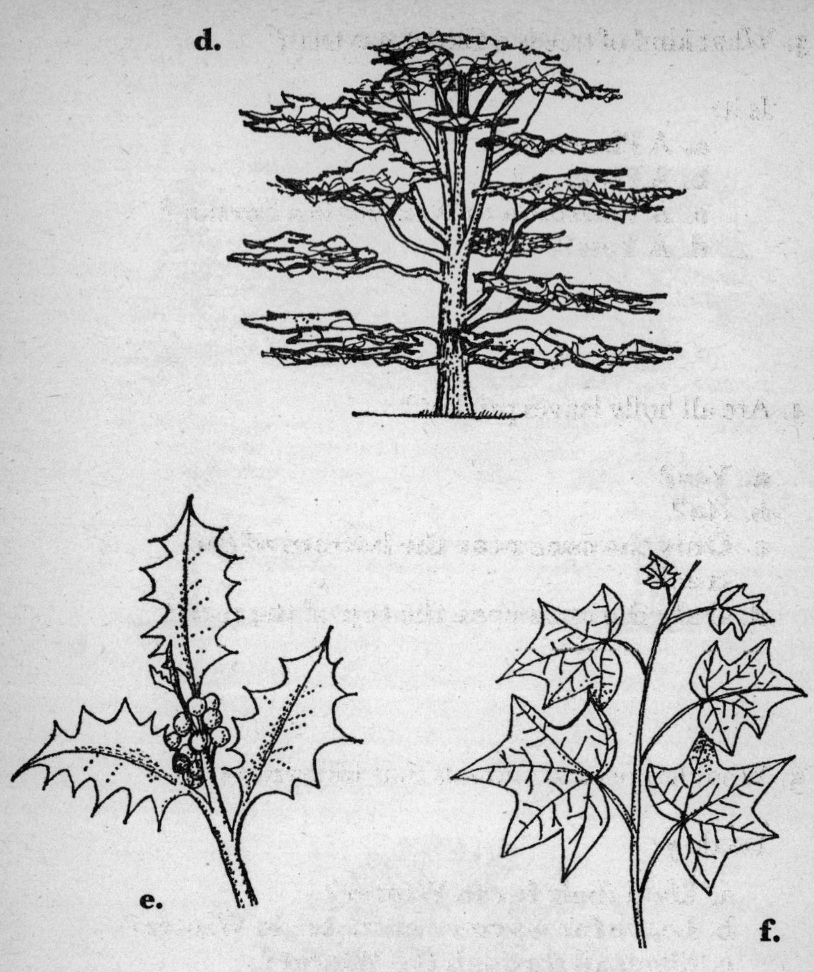



Can you name them?

**3.** What kind of tree is a Christmas tree?

Is it:
- **a. A Pine tree?**
- **b. A Fir tree?**
- **c. A Common or Norwegian Spruce?**
- **d. A Yew?**

**4.** Are all holly leaves prickly?

- **a. Yes?**
- **b. No?**
- **c. Only the ones near the bottom of the tree?**
- **d. Only the ones near the top of the tree?**

**5.** What happens to animals that **hibernate?**

Do they:
- **a. Shed their fur in Winter?**
- **b. Leave for warmer climates in Winter?**
- **c. Sleep all through the Winter?**
- **d. Live underground in Winter?**

**6.** Of the animals in this list, which ones hibernate?

**Snakes**
**Toads**
**Snails**
**Hedgehogs**
**Rats**
**Moles**
**Frogs**
**Badgers**
**Stoats**
**Dormice**
**Weasels**
**Ferrets**
**Lizards**
**Worms**
**Cows**
**Bats**
**Foxes**
**Voles**

**7.** Here are thirteen small birds that will stay in the British Isles throughout Winter:

102

c.
d.
e.
f.
g.
h.

How many of them can you name?

 These are two very pretty yellow flowers that you find growing in wintertime. One of them is a Celandine and one is a Winter Aconite:

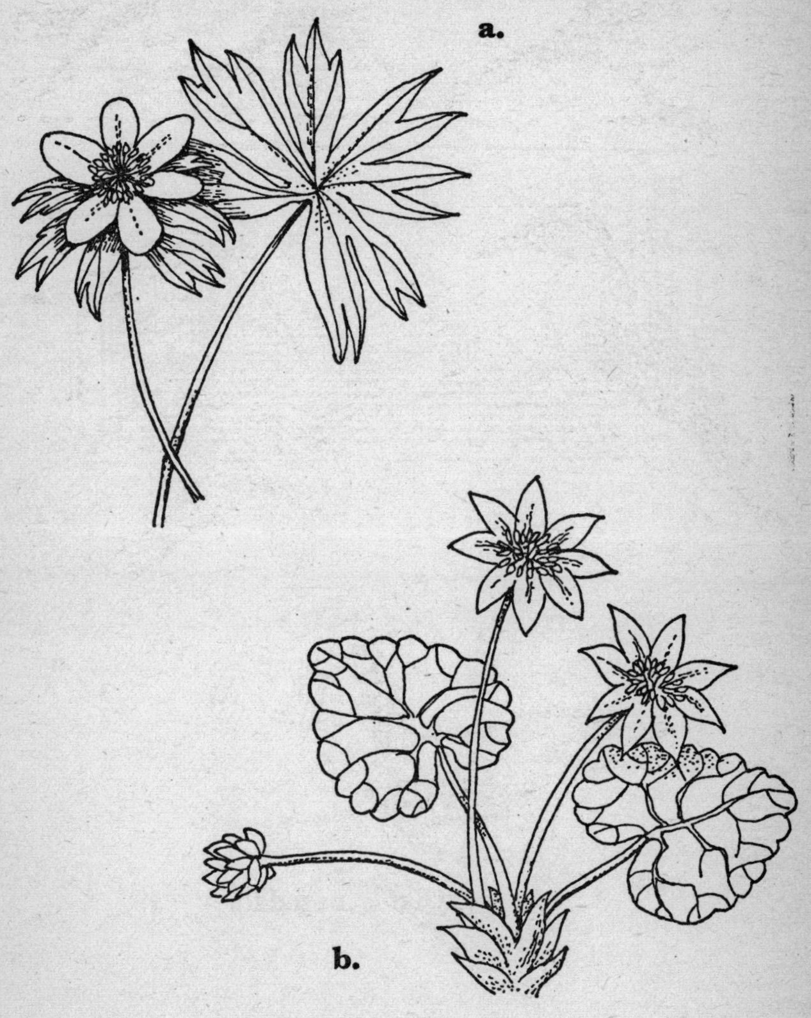



But which is which?

**9.** What's this:

And what is it used for?

**10.** Here are two kinds of mice that you will find in the country in Winter:

Can you name them?

**11.** And here are three kinds of vole that you will find in the country in Winter:

Naming the voles isn't as easy as naming the mice, but can you do it?

**12.** Here are three kinds of shrew you will find in the
country in Winter:

If you were able to name the mice *and* the voles,
you must know your country animals very well.
Can you name the three kinds of shrew?

**13.** Here are the names of thirteen flowers:

> **Snowdrop**
> **Shepherd's Purse**
> **Lousewort**
> **Rock Rose**
> **Groundsel**
> **Speedwell**
> **Pansy**
> **Red Clover**
> **Dandelion**
> **Deadnettle**
> **Harebell**
> **Primrose**
> **Lily**

Six of the flowers are ones you might see in the country in late Winter. Can you spot the six?

And can you recognise them from the drawings below and on the next page?

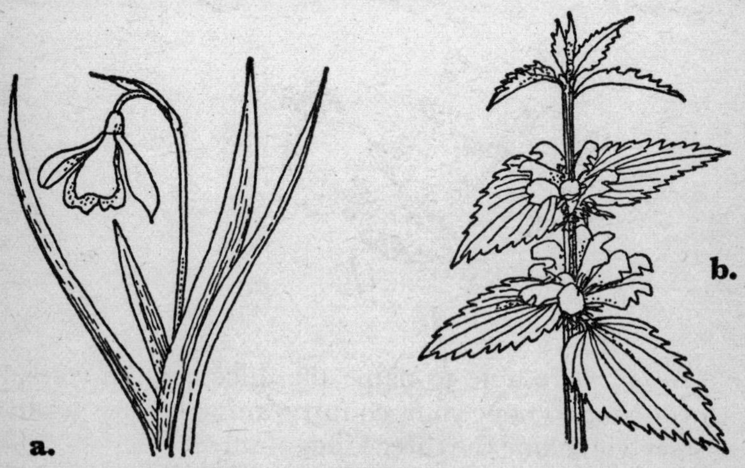

a.

b.

c.
d.
e.
f.

**14.** Look carefully at the drawing of this bird:

A flock of these birds flying over a field is something you quite often see in Winter. What are the birds called?

Are they:

      **a. Lapwings?**
      **b. Peewits?**
      **c. Green Plovers?**

Can you name them?

**16.** Here are the names of six kinds of Tit:

> **Great Tit**
> **Coal Tit**
> **Marsh Tit**
> **Long-tailed Tit**
> **Crested Tit**
> **Bearded Tit**

And here are pictures of them:

a.

b.

Can you name each
Tit correctly?

And do you know which other Tit is also known as
a Tom Tit?

**17.** Which animal changes the colour of its coat in Winter:

Is it:

> **The Water Rat?**
> **The Stoat?**
> **The Dormouse?**
> **The Red Squirrel?**
> **The Chameleon?**

And **why** does it change the colour of its
coat in Winter?
And **where** in the British Isles can you see
this happening?
And **which** are the colours that change
and **what** do they change to?

To help you, here is a picture of the animal before
its colours have begun to change:

**18.** Here is the tree from which the pussy-willow comes:

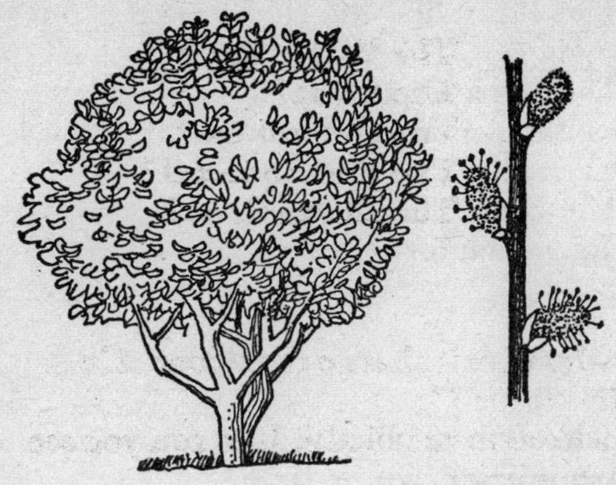

What is the tree called?

**19.** Here is something that is sometimes called a lamb's tail:

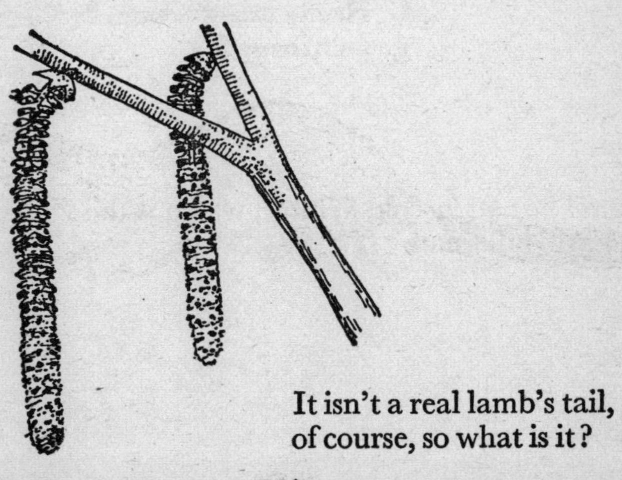

It isn't a real lamb's tail, of course, so what is it?

**20.** Why do you often see birds following a farmer's tractor? It is because:

**a.** The birds like the noise of the tractor?

**b.** The birds like the fumes of the tractor's engine?

**c.** The birds hope that the farmer is sowing seed and that they will be able to pick up the seed as soon as he has scattered it?

**d.** The birds can catch the worms and grubs the plough turns up?

**21.** Which of these jobs would you expect to see a farmer doing in winter time?

Would it be:

**a.** Harvesting swedes?
**b.** Sowing corn?
**c.** Ploughing?
**d.** Haymaking?
**e.** Hedging?
**f.** Harvesting wheat?
**g.** Lambing?

**22.** If it is a *very* cold Winter, which is the squirrel that will hibernate?

**23.** Once upon a time there was a man who spent much of the Winter grinding grain. What was he called?

**24.** Once upon a time windmills and water mills were used right through the winter. What were they used for?

# Little Trotty Wagtail

*Little trotty wagtail, he went in the rain,*
*And twittering, tottering sideways he ne' er got straight*
  *again.*
*He stooped to get a worm, and looked up to get a fly.*
*And then he flew away ere his feathers they were dry.*

*Little trotty wagtail, he waddled in the mud,*
*And left his little footmarks, trample where he would.*
*He waddled in the water-pudge, and waggle went his*
  *tail,*
*And chirrupt up his wings to dry upon the garden rail.*

*Little trotty wagtail, you nimble all about,*
*And in the dimpling water-pudge you waddle in and out;*
*Your home is nigh at hand, and in the warm pig-stye,*
*So, little Master Wagtail, I'll bid you a good-bye.*

**John Clare**

# Answers to the Winter Quiz

1. They do not shed their leaves in Winter.
2. 
   - **a. Pine**   **b. Fir**
   - **c. Yew**   **d. Cedar**
   - **e. Holly**   **f. Ivy**
3. **A Common or Norwegian Spruce**
4. Only the ones near the bottom of the tree.
5. They sleep all through the Winter.
6. 

| | |
|---|---|
| **Snakes** | **Lizards** |
| **Toads** | **Frogs** |
| **Dormice** | **Snails** |
| **Hedgehogs** | **Bats** |

7. 
   - **a. Skylark**   **b. Rock Pipit**
   - **c. Pied Wagtail**   **d. Stonechat**
   - **e. Starling**   **f. Mistle Thrush**
   - **g. Song Thrush**   **h. Robin**
   - **i. Sparrows**   **j. Nuthatch**
   - **k. Woodpecker**   **l. Kingfisher**
   - **m. Wren**
8. 
   - **a.** is a **Winter Aconite**
   - **b.** is a **Celandine**
9. It is a cattle grid, consisting of metal bars placed over a hollow pit, so that cattle are afraid to walk over it, but people can.
10. **a. Harvest Mouse**   **b. Woodmouse**
11. **a. Short-tailed Vole**   **b. Water Vole**
    **c. Bank Vole**
12. **a. Common Shrew**   **b. Water Shrew**
    **c. Pygmy Shrew**
13. 
    - **a. Snowdrop**   **b. Deadnettle**
    - **c. Shepherd's Purse**   **d. Speedwell**
    - **e. Dandelion**   **f. Groundsel**

**14.** The bird is a **Lapwing** and **Lapwings** are also known as **Peewits** and **Green Plovers**!

**15.** a. **Blackbird**  b. **Crow**  c. **Rook**

**16.** a. **Great Tit**  b. **Coal Tit**
c. **Bearded Tit**  d. **Marsh Tit**
e. **Long-tailed Tit**  f. **Crested Tit**
The **Blue Tit** is also known as **Tom Tit.**

**17.** In Winter the **Stoat** changes from brown and white to pure white so that it becomes invisible on snow-covered ground. This is rarely seen in England and Wales, but common on the Scottish Highlands.

**18.** **The Sallow** or **Goat Willow**

**19.** **A Catkin**

**20.** The birds can catch the worms and grubs the plough turns up.

**21.** **Ploughing, hedging,** and, in some areas only, **lambing.**

**22.** **The Red Squirrel**

**23.** **A Miller**

**24.** **Grinding grain**

**Answer to the Question on page 98**
A tree!

# COUNTRY CODE

## Leave No Litter—Take It Home

All litter is unsightly, and some is dangerous as well. In the country, cans and broken bottles are a hazard to livestock. So are plastic bags and wrappers; cows or sheep will eat them all too readily, not realising that pain and even death may result.

The countryside is not well supplied with litter bins. But paper and plastic wrappers, cigarette packets, cans and bottles which have been brought there can as easily be taken back home or to other places where a disposal service can more conveniently be provided.

So set aside a bag for picnic debris, keep a litter container in the car. Better still, always try to bring back just a bit more litter than you yourself produced.

## Guard Against All Risk of Fire

It's all too easy to be a fire-raiser in the country. Matches or cigarette ends thrown away while still alight, pipes carelessly knocked out against a tree, broken bottles or jars left where the sun can turn them into burning glasses—any one of these could devastate acres of woodland, moorland or forest, killing animals and birds and leaving a disfigured landscape which takes years to recover.

Most forests are planned for at very least twenty years' growth. One person's off-guard moment could easily start a fire accounting for thousands of years of tree growth. It's a sobering thought. As the Australians say—and their bush fires give them good cause to know—'One flaming match, no flaming trees.'

## Fasten All Gates

You can't tell a cow to stay where it's put. Sheep are notorious for straying and for following one another. That's why the farmer fences his stock into his fields. Neither he nor his neighbours want to spend their time rounding up cows or sheep from fields of crops where these animals could easily gorge themselves to death, or from roads where they could cause serious accidents. Where it is necessary to move animals from one field to another or across roads, the farmer puts a gate which can be closed. And it should normally stay closed unless it is in use.

## Keep Dogs under Proper Control

Farmers have good reason to regard visiting dogs as pests. In the country a civilised town dog can become a savage and cause a lot of damage by chasing animals just for the fun of it. In sheep-farming areas even an innocent dog may be helping to spread disease if it is allowed to run loose.

Nor it is just the farm animals that are at risk. Dogs caught worrying livestock may be shot and their owners may have to pay heavy compensation. Keep your dog above suspicion, under proper control at all times, and on the lead wherever there is livestock about.

## Avoid Damaging Fences, Hedges and Walls

Maintaining fences, hedges and walls is an expensive business. When you have to make good the damage resulting from the carelessness or impatience of strangers it is more than expensive—it is infuriating. So keep on the right side of farmers and landowners—and their fences. Cross by the gates or stiles provided; if you stick to the paths you shouldn't find that fences get in your way.

## Keep to Paths Across Farmland

Even a few pairs of feet can do a lot of harm to crops. Growth is held up, and harvesting is harder when corn or hay is trodden flat or lain upon. Shakespeare's 'pretty country folks' had the good sense to lie 'between the acres of the rye'.

Remember too that what may seem to be just 'long grass' is really a crop. Damage to it may mean that cows or sheep go hungry next winter.

When paths cross fields or follow field edges, help them to keep their shape by walking single file, country style.

## Safeguard Water Supplies

Water is becoming a more valuable commodity all the time. Most of what we use is collected originally by run-off from the countryside, often from just those hills and valleys which are attractive to the motorist, the walker, the camper and caravanner. And a country stream may provide a direct local water supply for people and animals.

Be careful to avoid the sort of pollution that can arise from rubbish tipped into streams, or from inadequate sanitary arrangements when camping. Remember too that water is vital to livestock, and never interfere with cattle troughs.

## Go Carefully on Country Roads

Driving on country roads requires as much care and attention as driving in towns. Around the next blind corner, hidden by high banks or hedges, could be any one of the special country hazards; slow-moving tractors, mud on the road, farm animals, parties of walkers or cyclists.

Motorists should reduce their speed, particularly where roads are narrow; walkers should keep to the right, facing oncoming traffic, where there is no footpath.

Care and consideration by car owners can help ensure that our cars don't spoil the countryside. Keep to the roads, and off commons, bridleways and green lanes, and beaches. Avoid, too, parking so as to block entry to fields or farm premises.

## Protect Wild Life, Wild Plants and Trees

Wild life in Britain is under attack from many sides—from pesticides, pollution and destruction of habitat. To pick or uproot flowers, carve or otherwise damage trees, and to disturb wild animals and birds only makes their survival harder. So does collecting: most naturalists nowadays learn to study plants and animals in their natural habitat—not in collections.

Nature is a network—a web of animals and plants depending on one another. The pattern changes with the seasons, and through the years as new species evolve and old disappear. But, as man is finding out, the overall stability is maintained by having many different species. So in our own interests we must try to disturb the pattern as little as possible.

In the country you are part of this vital, natural but fragile community; drive delicately, tread softly and walk warily.

## Respect the Life of the Countryside

Townspeople visiting the countryside are sometimes regarded with suspicion by the natives. There may well be good reason for this. If earlier visitors, unaware of the Country Code, have put farmers and others to inconvenience or expense, it may be years before the damage to good town-and-country relations is repaired.

So avoid the kind of unneighbourly behaviour which fosters prejudice. Remember that noise travels far, particularly from portable or car radios loudly played, and is annoying not only to those who live in the country but also to those who have gone there to enjoy its peace and quiet.

Respect for the life of the countryside also means understanding the nature of the work that goes on there. In other industries capital equipment and stores are locked up and guarded when not in use. But farm machinery often has to stand out of doors and un-protected, while hay and other crops may be stored in open barns or stacks. The public is on trust, and it is up to all of us to make sure that this trust is not misplaced.

**Follow the Country Code**
Guard against all risk of fire
Fasten all gates
Keep dogs under proper control
Avoid damaging fences, hedges and walls
Keep to the paths across farmland
Leave no litter
Safeguard water supplies
Protect wild life, wild plants and trees
Go carefully on country roads
Respect the life of the countryside

*Prepared by the Countryside Commission and the Central
Office of Information 1971*

If you would like to receive a newsletter telling you
about our new children's books, fill in the coupon
with your name and address and send it to:

Gillian Osband,
Transworld Publishers Ltd,
Century House,
61–63 Uxbridge Road, Ealing,
London, W5 5SA

NAME ................................................................

ADDRESS ...........................................................

....................................................................

....................................................................

CHILDREN'S NEWSLETTER

All the books on the previous pages are available at your bookshop or can be
ordered direct from Transworld Publishers Ltd., Cash Sales Dept., P.O. Box
11, Falmouth, Cornwall.
Please send full name and address together with cheque or postal order—no
currency, and allow 22p per book to cover postage and packing (plus 10p
each for additional copies).